Hip Hop Dance

Hip Hop Dance

Meanings and Messages

Carla Stalling Huntington

McFarland & Company, Inc., Publishers
Jefferson, North Carolina, and London

LIBRARY OF CONGRESS CATALOGUING-IN-PUBLICATION DATA

Huntington, Carla Stalling, 1961–
    Hip hop dance : meanings and messages / Carla Stalling
Huntington.
       p.   cm.
    Includes bibliographical references and index.

    ISBN-13: 978-0-7864-2991-2
    (softcover : 50# alkaline paper) ∞

    1. Hip-Hop dance.   2. Hip-hop dance — Social aspects.
I. Title.
GV1796.H57H86 2007
793.3–dc22   2007004867

British Library cataloguing data are available

Cover photograph ©2007 BananaStock

Manufactured in the United States of America

*McFarland & Company, Inc., Publishers
  Box 611, Jefferson, North Carolina 28640
   www.mcfarlandpub.com*

For Mother Louise and Mother Lucille

Acknowledgments

There are many people that I would like to thank, and I hope I do not leave anyone out.

First there is Dr. Paul Gelles. He was a professor of mine in graduate school, in an anthropology seminar. Dr. Gelles was the first one to give me the idea that what I had to write about with regard to this topic was interesting and valuable. He encouraged me, led me, in the writing of papers and on this topic.

Dr. Jacqueline Shea Murphy was most instrumental as well. She was one of my professors in the Dance Department at the University of California, Riverside. From her I learned that my work had value too, but also that writing is a process, an important process. I still have recollections of the writing seminar that I took with her, and of what I learned about writing. She suggested that I print out pages and arrange them on the floor, so that I could move them around and see what fit. I thought it was absurd at first. Now I do it as part of the process I use in writing anything at all.

Next comes Dr. Anna B. Scott. I was deeply impressed with her. She was the first person that I encountered who put Marx and Capitalism in the studio. It was great. She was not afraid, and I learned from her more than I can comfortably articulate here.

My friend Dr. Judith Turian was influential and continues to be. She provided encouragement when I felt like throwing in the disks and saying, "Forget this book, who cares anyway?" She lovingly encouraged me to keep at it and helped me to move beyond my fears.

Carolyn Frederick did wonders, too. She understood that in order to write a book like this, one had to be, well, an artist. I love her for sharing the excitement with me.

Dolores Reece: thank you for years and years of encouragement in the process of soaring.

Dr. Susan Foster was very instrumental in this work. It was in talking with her that I found the ability to do what a feminine feminist can do, to move beyond certain belief systems or at least examine them before swallowing.

The ArtsBridge Program at the University of California, Riverside, and their participating Harrison Elementary School faculty, staff, and students enabled me to teach hip hop dance and history simultaneously, keeping language, history, and danced texts tied together. I appreciate all the children who participated, though I cannot list them all here.

Dr. Sally A. Ness helped me to write.

Bre Dance Studio and Theater and the dancers there were terrific in helping me with observational data. It is one of the few African American owned dance studios in Southern California.

Finally to Rennie Harris; Ben Reid, Jr.; Donald and Alma Johnson; Doris-Owanda Johnson; Belinda Johnson; my son Donald; my spiritual teachers; The Golden Dawn and my Inner Being.

Thank you.

Table of Contents

Preface

Many stereotypes circulate about black dance. Black dance has been read and written about since the African Diaspora. And in many cases, black dance, has been seen, over time, as a way for "those people" to express their feelings, be they good, bad, or indifferent. Moreover, black dance, once learned by mainstream culture, provides for some sort of identity creation for the dancer learning the dance; and perhaps by vicarious associations, onlookers who watch dances done by whites that were once black dance allow for yet another expressive representation of the symbiotic relationships between blacks and whites.

Hip hop dance is one aspect of black/African American hip hop culture that has been through some of these processes by circulating through global cultures, providing meanings for those of mainstream culture, but also providing something for others who find themselves caught up in the capitalist machinery of production and profits. This book examines hip hop dance as text, as a commentary, and as a function of identity construction within the confines of consumerism. The book also provides a reading of hip hop dance and social positioning of African Americans from a black feminist point of view, and documents the commoditization and codification of the dance.

Providing theoretical and critical analysis of hip hop dance, the arguments demonstrate that this African American dance form has scholarly credence and value. Tracing the dance from the Diaspora to the dance floor, this book covers a social history germane not only to

1

the African American experience, but also to the global experience of laborers who learn lessons from hip hop dance. The book draws on popular cultural images from films, commercials, and dance studios, as well as on global observational research, to set forth the theory of hip hop dance and its use in a capitalist agenda. Comparing the codification of hip hop dance to ballet supports ideology that forces equalization of the high and low.

The dance form covered in these pages has not been discussed in this manner before. What is important therefore is to understand the simultaneous roles played and nuances found in hip hop dance in the larger social framework of American culture, and how today it is used and re-created for ends that differ from the intentions of the dance at its nascence. In addition, it is important to see the ways in which the meanings and messages given in the African American dance language translate for other groups of people around the globe who find their environments less than ideal.

The book begins with an introduction to dance scholarship and hip hop dance. Then it moves into identifying the connections between hip hop dance and the African Diaspora. From there, the book engages a feminist reading of the social issues confronting blacks and the use of the dance to address some of them. In the remaining chapters, consumption and consumer behavior are covered from the perspective of the dance being a commodity. This part of the book includes a discussion of global movement of the dance and postmodernism, and the ways in which the codification of the dance in the United States occurred. The epilogue briefly discusses what still needs to be theorized and researched, and reflects on the lessons of the book. It is hoped that the reader will come away with a broader understanding of the weight and depth of the dance text and a historical understanding of its necessity and value.

Introduction

"The association of words with dance has a long history that goes back to precolonial West African empires ... dance can be understood as a form of orality."

— Francesca Castaldi, *Choreographies of African Identities* (2006, 4)

I know hip hop dance when I see it but it cannot be touched. It can be described, sold, and transmitted; learned, choreographed and commoditized. Used. Profited from.

However, hip hop dance writes, theorizes, interprets, and communicates.

This rich, wondrous text, once written but then not theorizing, interpreting or communicating, finds distribution through television commercials and programs, commercial films, music videos, instructional videos, at concerts, in commercial dance studios, at cheerleading and marching band locales, online, in graphic and cartoon form, and in private consumption spaces. These points of intake cater to a diverse set of people who come from many divisions of life.

One finds housewives wanting to learn, suburban youth identifying with its misinterpreted messages and meanings, Indians, Asians, Australians, Europeans, Africans, Euro American whites, African Americans and many in between who want to too. Learning not in the streets of inner city ghettos but in suburban studios whose products include

Introduction

1) every-child-gets-a-feel-good-about-him-or-herself-medal won at a hip hop dance competition even if they cannot dance and; 2) recital numbers seen by proud yet uneasy parents where the youngsters shake behinds and stand like non-threatening original gangsters they saw on JC Penney commercials for back to school clothes.

And moreover, some of those who do not overtly engage in learning the dance are themselves often intrigued at the sheer athleticism of the text. I have witnessed middle-aged white women trying out the moves behind the closed doors of empty but adjacent dance studio spaces when they think no one is looking and their children are taking class. They laughed embarrassedly when they saw me looking at them trying to do The Runnin' Man. They said it was better than aerobics. I smiled and nodded with them in agreement.

Why the deep connect with hip hop dance? What strength does it bring? What understanding does it possess? Is it because it is inherently an African American cultural artifact that has succeeded in its export in becoming more American than African? Is it because it is cool and to be American is to be a cool cultural consumption cat? What about it being movement that Others[1] can learn and do? In fact, from a social identity point of view, hip hop dance provides something for almost everyone.[2] A piece of identity that is as portable as a digital game player, a Blackberry, and a personal digital assistant. A remnant of hip hop dance resides in many around the globe, from those who actively or passively shun it to those who consume it directly or indirectly. In this way the connection between hip hop dance and consumption results from the Cabbaging of artifact and historical texts to create the quintessential Patch. It has Bounced from the characterization of the Snake described black man to the Popped Locks embodying resistance to capitalism and the notions promising you can have it your way. More Runnin' Men (and women) have been seen in America and abroad as jobs have gone overseas and as developing geographies are exploited for labor.

Hip hop dance itself is cool, rowdy, defiant, sexy, athletic, smooth, creative. It is also full of meaning — meaning that kind of meaning attributable to ethnographic and cultural contexts.[3] Meanings metabolize in the distribution channel and at points of consumption, when the dance is codified and made into a commodity, used as a medium of value. And so, herein lies the purpose of this book: to bring hip hop dance texts into focus so that a certain set of meanings is documented. I liken this book to a museum function and a social history for the dance, providing a hermeneutical method of preservation, through my observations, research, and experiences.

As hip hop dance comes across the screen no tangible named authors of the text exist.[4] But the text is real. It is my view that the history written by the texts of hip hop dance is on the way to being lost in the commercialization, globalization, codification, and commoditization processes. Many have vested interests in these processes. Videographers, product manufacturers, sports cartels, multinational corporations, commercial choreographers, consumers, rappers, and dance studio owners represent only some of the stakeholders who benefit materially from the dissemination of dance texts devoid of meaning and author. The problem with saluting these vested interests, in my opinion, is that doing so limits recognition of hip hop dance as an art form, a written document, and cultural artifact. As it is currently being distributed around the globe, it reminds me of the mass reproduction of, for example, clay pottery art. The purpose of such production is merely for consumption and profit. Those who create the art are often powerless to effect change over the machination. While I may not be able to arrest the processes, I can set forth ideology that sees the dance as text containing historical information that can be read and communicated. These points deserve acknowledgement and preservation, regardless.

Hip hop dance is a black social dance offering texts that deliver strategic and tactical ways of being in the world and remembering worlds past. They contain metaphors and theories about existence and the life of the dancers collectively and individually, and the social fabric we are webbed with. There are macro- and micro-social, political and economic structures of Signification present in these dances begging exploration.[5] For example, in addition to the processes I discussed above, black feminism and hip hop dance have been under-theorized and under-deployed in looking at the currents on which related tactics, metaphors, and theories travel. Moreover, hip hop dance utilizes the choreographed text of US Ebonics for its writing.[6] (I will refer to US Ebonics as Ebonics hereafter for convenience.) However, Ebonics is situated as a spoken language given informal recognition only when one is being a cool consumption cat as such, because now it ain't cool to speak proper American English. Ebonics, though, is a language which nevertheless carries with it Signification. As you can see, there is a lot going on with hip hop dance, and I am just getting started.

* * *

In her article *The Race for Theory*, Barbara Christian (1999) acknowledged that in certain academic circles, the creation, production, and publication of a theory of something has supplanted development of discussion and publication of ideas and literature. The marketability of a theory and its acceptance has, further, forced writers wanting publication and academic advancement to use the theories. Silence seems the only suitable alternative. And of course some of the theories, in my view and apparently in Christian's too, are flatly absurd. Political circles and other constraints prevent stating the obvious though. With regard to writing styles, she suggested that some theoretical writing was poorly constructed and difficult to read. Clearly not all academic writing that is produced in their publications comes across that way. However, because this is the conventional wisdom in academia, writing styles adhere to a certain format if the writing is to be published and considered scholarly. I am sure you can think of several authors whose writing is atrocious and difficult to read, that have set forth a theory that is downright hard to believe, yet validated and valued nevertheless.

I have made several decisions in writing this book. First of all, I want it to be accessible to a number of readers, if I can be so bold as to think a number of readers will want to read this book. I also want to engage academia in this. It is important to me that this book invite readers, whatever their affiliation, to reflect on how to make sense out of hip hop dance, and what it means for their lives and those around them. And to go 'head on with what they want to do.

Consider what bell hooks writes in regard to this in *Teaching to Transgress* (1994). Importantly she says we have to use the accepted language to write and be published, even if it is the oppressor's language (1994, 169). In talking about black feminist theory, she points out the difficulty in intellectualizing it on the one hand, and the complexity of living it on the other. This is not to stop us though from writing or theorizing. Going on, she indicates writing is "most meaningful when it invites readers to engage in critical reflection ... to make sense out of life and the lives of others" (70). In so doing, hooks believes in engaging and including a wide readership base in broad locations. That choice however is not without consequences. She warns, "to reach as many readers as possible in as many different locations" is a risk to academic rewards because the decision produces criticism, labels, and judgments of her work. From academia the gavel pounds on the desk in its sentencing of people's contributions that do not cut the mustard: "not scholarly enough" and "not theoretical" (1994, 71). I am afraid of this and yet have decided to follow my own course nevertheless.

A moment ago I said there is a great deal going on with hip hop dance. I cannot address every aspect of it here. I do theorize the dance, present a feminist point of view and talk about its consumption relative to economics and its consumption relative to identity. The way that I go about this ranges from macro to micro and back and forth. I also consider Ebonics as a language that has been denied legitimacy. I have to tell you now that my writing is tainted with being an African-Cuban American, born and raised in Los Angeles, colored with my education as an economist, business woman, dance practitioner, historian and theorist. Influenced by my efforts in learning, performing, choreographing and teaching ballet and hip hop dance. Constrained by mothering, wifing, and defying. Mediated by working with established colonial structures, jaundiced by men, filtered by hurt and life experiences, and not least of all, slanted by the institutions of publishing and academia.

It is my hope that you, the reader, will find something you can use constructively from reading this book that will help you make sense of life, aid in your understanding of hip hop dance, or encourage you to move, grow, and challenge. The format of the book does not follow the hip hop dance kind of rhythm. As you know already, there are footnotes. I do not use Ebonics extensively in writing the text but some phrases are used for emphasis. A preface and epilogue surround the chapters. The form of the book is regular; it does not try to dance or stage a show. Some lofty, many-lettered words are used but for the most part I try to keep that under control. Most importantly, I am here not dead.

I focus on the dance and not the music. Rap and hip hop music have received theoretical attention from many scholars. I could make a laundry list of the different scholars from the fields of cultural, ethnic, African American, and women's studies; and ethnomusicology and anthropology. To find these, all one has to do is connect to one's favorite search engine and type in rap, rappers, rap music, or other indexed words like them, and a plethora of material will be available at the click of a mouse. That is not so much the case with hip hop dance. And when thinking about why that is, I imagine that is because the dance has been separated from the music (language) in a feminizing, maybe trivializing, fashion.[7]

About rap music hooks theorized that "in contemporary black popular culture, rap music has become one of the spaces where black vernacular speech is used in a manner that invites dominant mainstream culture to listen" (1994, 171). By textualizing hip hop dance and what it theorizes I hope by virtue of this volume, to reduce its trivialization and to create a space where the dance is not feminized but rather seen for the value it holds at the multifaceted and complex nexuses where cultures and markets interact.

I am not going to recreate or restate work that has already been done about African American dance, for example work that documents the notion of being cool while dancing, cotillions that excluded black men while sales of black women to Euro-American men took place, the development of black social dance through jookin, honky-tonks and rent parties, or what it meant to perform in Black Face during minstrelsy, dance the Lindy Hop and so on. Plenty of excellent and able scholars have covered that territory and have made outstanding contributions to the history of African American dance, and its relation to African, Brazilian, and Caribbean dance.[8] I also refrain from giving you a history of Africa and African dance, again because many scholars have taken up these issues. Having given you this caveat, I do use some work related to the African Diaspora to drive home points, to situate, and to add salience. I do discuss some works that I believe are germane to my purposes here in regard to hip hop dance, and texts that are relevant in areas of semiotics, dance theory, and consumption.

Before I go any further: Please know that I focus on African Americans, using my personal experiences and observations, images circulating in popular culture, and sources of academic and non–academic literature to formulate my arguments and theories. Also know that I am absolutely mindful of other groups of people who have experienced racism and social difficulties as groups and individuals: those with alternative sexual lifestyles, people with AIDS/HIV, Jews, Middle Easterners, Hispanics, Chinese, Japanese, Native Americans, Aborigines, and so on. I do not want to essentialize. Additionally, this work is purely mine in the sense that it is not an empirical research project, nor a product of a dissertation, not the funded research of a foundation, not a publication required for me to get tenure. It is not testing a hypothesis or trying to develop a corner on the hip hop dance literature market.

Why did I write this book? I guess the first question should be why did I want to write this book? The answers to these two questions are not simple or separable. I think it was because of my father. He was the first person I danced with, learning the Cha-Cha and other Caribbean dances in the living room back in Philly, listening to records he played on the hi-fi he'd made. Actually it could be because of my mother. She used to dance with us — me and my two sisters — in the living room over there in The Jungle. Or maybe it was because of Kurt Washington. We won the dance contest in junior high. We did the Bump and, boy, let me tell you, we were good, dancing to *Fopp* by the Ohio Players (1974). No, that wasn't the song. I can't remember now exactly. But Mom has a picture of us on the guest bedroom nightstand. It could be the Rodney King riots (I could not believe that *sister-girl* was looting) or the OJ trial. Maybe it was my son and the inevitable problems with being a black male being raised by a perpetually single black female and the effect hip hop dance had on him. By that time I was teaching him how to dance at home, but we were also doing Street Jazz, a formal class where the neighborhood folks could learn. I had moved out of Los Angeles then.

It could be simply that I am a child of the hip hop generation, one who danced in the streets and at house parties to the Sugarhill Gang on and on till the break of dawn (Rhino Records Inc., 1999) and *(Not Just) Knee Deep*, Funkadelic (Rhino Records, Inc., 1994) waving my hands in the air like ... looking for the *Flashlight* (Parliament 2006 redistribution).

My desire to write this book certainly could have been due to experiences in corporate America. My head still hurts from bumping up against that glass ceiling, and swimming from the realization that working class has expanded greatly: three paychecks from homeless *is* three paychecks from homeless, whether you work on the frontline or are responsible for the bottom line. They make you think you can be like the wealthy, and maybe you can, but I couldn't. Mostly because to get wealthy, except for playing the lotto, or going down there to the casino where they give the Native Americans a bone, or inheriting a lot of money (which as you and I know for most of us isn't exactly likely), you have to usually be a capitalist, which I, for damn sure, don't have the stomach for. Besides, I was tired of being called all out of my name: uppity and intimidating.

Actually when you get right down to it, I knew I wanted to write this book plus others after I was in the fourth grade in elementary school. But it wasn't until I got to graduate school that I got material to read to start making sense of the world which freed me to be a feminine black feminist who can do hip hop dance and ballet, and read and write research in consumption practices. Some how it was then that I remembered that Mother Louise was a Tuskegee graduate in chemistry, and Grandfather was a doctor from a historically black college. That Uncle was a big shot superintendent of a huge public school, but something happened and I felt the burden. It was in graduate school where I got the courage to do this, and other things that I had not been able to do. It was there that I re-evaluated marriage, religion, consumption, and the American Dream. That courage remains with me and on the pages of this book.

A moment of silence....

I am grateful that you are engaging with this work.

The African American hip hop dances that I theorize generally came out of the 14-year period between 1985 to 2001 and are categorized, thanks to Katrina Hazzard-Donald's apt analysis in her 1996 essay in *Droppin' Science*, as Rap Dance, House Dance and Concert Dance (from here out I now collectively refer to these as hip hop dance). However, not all African American hip hop dances coming out of that period of time are discussed. The hip hop dances that I have selected tend to have been popular amongst social dancers, and many of them are recognized around the globe, in media and commercial representations, and have been or are being codified. I deal directly with hip hop dance codification in the last chapter of this book.

It is important to know the history of African American dance, and how to trace it from Africa to the Caribbean to Brazil to North America. But I want to press and reinforce a connection between them, or stated differently, press for intertextuality such that the history of African Americans in the United States has brought us hip hop dance. So I am not going to recreate a linear origin but rely instead on the intertextuality of African and African American social dances. That approach allows one to move away from placing an origin on everything. It is a piecing together of different parts to come up with a theory such that "intertextuality represents a process of repetition and revision ... [of] shared structural elements that suggest familiarity with other texts" (Gates 1988, 60).[9]

In regard to the spread of hip hop dance as commodity Anna B. Scott made an excellent contribution entitled "Dance" in 2001 to *Culture Works*. In her chapter she discusses the commercialization of black dance, black bodies and black souls, and other related issues. Reading

Scott's text is, for me, like walking down a safe street, looking good on a not too hot day with a few clouds and plenty of sun, when you have enough money to pay your bills and have some left over for some chips and an Icee, you're in a good relationship with all the people in your family *and* your man, you got a legitimate job and your body don't hurt nowhere. Her text does what hooks and Christian spoke of. Scott eloquently encourages readers of African American dance, and hip hop dance by extension, to understand the implications of the "relationships of the components of a 'dance event' that are often not regarded as vital to the dance, but are in fact integral to the execution and evaluation of African Diaspora performance" (2001, 108). That point is one that needs to be in the forefront throughout the entire reading of this book. When I talk about commercials and marketing that use hip hop dance I will return to Scott.

Francesca Castaldi has recently published *Choreographies of African Identities: Negritude, Dance and the National Ballet of Senegal* (2006). In this work Castaldi presents her ethnographic field work studying a ballet from Senegal but wherein we learn, among other important aspects, that the association of words with dance has a long African history, a history that comes through, in my view, with hip hop dance. That dance is a form of writing rather than a simple movement that signifies macropolitcal processes. From her interpretation of her research, I was inspired to develop the following grand schema from her description of polyrhythms. Hip hop dance is comprised of writing, dance, and consumption as a non-restored behavior.[10] Then history or time if you will works on these as a crucible, its metamorphosis is made through a mortar and pestle leading to a commodity, a change in identity, a new theoretical meaning.

Using a different approach, Brenda Dixon Gottschild discusses many types of African American dance, including a brief mention of hip hop dance, in her 1996 *Digging the Africanist Presence in American Performance: Dance and Other Contexts*. This work mainly focuses on identifying Africanist influences on classical performing and fine arts. Her more recent *The Black Dancing Body: A Geography from Coon to Cool* (2005) positions the "black dancing body," and its significations over time within American mainstream culture through interviews with noted international performers and Gottschild's own historical interpretations. And of course there are dance theorists, many of whom will be discussed as I work, that include the topic of breakdancing in their research and theoretical publications. All of these and other writings about African American dance are critical to our understanding the social, economic and historical placement of African Americans over the past six centuries and the development of the dance form. These writers help convey a history that is relatively inclusive as well as give dance a respected place of study.

No doubt, accounts of African and African American dance almost always appear in some form or fashion in texts about slavery and the slave trade. *Scenes of Subjection: Terror, Slavery, and Self-Making in Nineteenth-Century America* by Saidiya V. Hartman (1997) is useful background material, and a very poignant and fascinating work. What Hartman explains is how the black body, through slavery and the Middle Passage, has been tortured and this torture misconstrued and manipulated into images that project both black people liking to dance and our supposed innate ability and affinity to enjoy being a commodity. Hartman explicitly argues that black dance was clandestinely used by the dancers and that it was not simply an amusement for slaves and masters and moreover, it was never a "natural" nor a "pastoral" activity. Positioning black dance this way was plain wrong, as we know. A fundamental premise therefore is that the "pained body" exists today, and seeks, is entitled to, "redress." However, remedy of the situation is not possible and the black body remembers the past while absorbing the pains of the present (1997, 77).

In addition to the discussion of the impossibility of redressing the pained black body, Hartman unpacks "performing blackness." This phrase

> conveys both the cross-purposes and the circulation of various modes of performance and performativity that concern the production of racial meaning and subjectivity, the nexus of race, subjection and spectacle, the forms of racial and race(d) pleasure, enactments of white dominance and power, and the reiteration and/or rearticulation of the conditions of enslavement [1997, 57].

I suggest that hip hop dance was connected to the Middle Passage in a cumulative memory at its inception, and that performing blackness has now been transposed in at least a bifurcated fashion onto bodies not necessarily black. On the one hand you have bodies that perform blackness because it is now cool. On the other hand, bodies learned to perform black precisely because of enslavement methods that occur globally. Learning is facilitated with the use of technology. Where does the black dancing body fit between these two poles now? I hope that by the time you have finished this book, that you have a satisfactory answer to this question.

As the reader may know, theories from other academic disciplines are used in dance historicizing because dance history is a newcomer to the academic construct. What I state about and how I use borrowed and applied theories reflects my own take, my own understanding and interpretation of what theories are saying. They provide useful ways of examining bodies and texts and give me a foundation on which I base some of my own theorizing. Several of these scholars I rely upon heavily, as you will see. Be warned however that my theories, conjectures, conclusions, postulates, and interpretations also rest upon non-scholarly non-fiction writers.

The book is divided into two parts. In Part I, the first chapter provides theoretical background and readings of bodily hip hop dance texts. Voice usage for this chapter is intended to be very scholarly and is written in the third person for the most part. The second chapter, using a more personal voice and the first person singular, links the African Diaspora and the Middle Passage with hip hop dance and language, and African American success. The third chapter provides a different view of the world from a feminist's perspective, again using personal experiences. Personal stories and observations, along with poignant quotes open each of these chapters. Part II changes tone with the start of the fourth chapter. It covers consumption and marketing, setting the stage for the next two chapters. The fifth chapter delves into how hip hop dance and related black body parts are used in pushing capitalist accumulation. These two chapters combine usage of the first and third person and include discussions and analyses of the use of hip hop dance in television commercials and marketing messages and the meanings of the new American Dream it conjures. The final chapter focuses on the codification and sale of hip hop dance as a commodity. I conclude the book with some thoughts about the process of writing this book, a synthesis of what I have learned, and the hope of what I would like to write about in the future.

Notes

1. Here, by *Other*, the reference is rhetorical, referring to those not located where hip hop dance had its nascence. Historically "Other" has been defined as non-white and ethnic, when the gaze has been anthropologically or colonially Euro- or Westerncentric. For more reading on these topics start with Hazzard-Donald 1996 and Castaldi 2006.

2. Social identity as it is used in this publication refers to that drawn from consumption as per R. Kleine, S.S. Kleine, and J. B. Kernan (1993). Those authors assert that consumption of any product or service is related to the self as a construct. The constructed self is projected and reinforced internally and externally, supported by objects of consumption. Kleine *et al* rely on J. P. Sartre's *Being and nothingness; A phenomenological essay on ontology*, New York Philosophical Library (1943/1956) wherein Sartre describes three states of existence — being, having, doing — to come to their conclusions. Social identity also resides in the beliefs, attitudes, and subjective norms a consumer has toward consuming a particular good or service. More of this is covered in a subsequent chapter. For further reading, please start with Ajzen and Fishbein 1980 and Madrigal 2001. This topic is taken up more fully later in the book in the chapter on consumption.

3. "Meaning is a perception or interpretation of an object. Meaning is not inherent in the object itself; rather it arises from the interaction of the individual, objects, and context, and it is inherently symbolic, subjective, psychological, and perceptual (Kleine and Kernan 1991, 312)."

4. Michel Foucault (1975) discusses, among other ideas about writers and texts, the relationship between a text and its writer, and how the text points to the writer who evidently stands outside the text and exists before the text does. The writer's name is associated with the text and conjures up the "status of the discourse within a society and culture" (147). However, one is only an author under certain conditions, including conditions of ownership, valorization, and appropriation, provided that these conditions are not usurped by indifference.

5. Here I am using the term Signification as part of the black vernacular semiotic process of Signifying after Gates (1988). The study of semiotics through noted writers such as Ferdinand de Saussure, Roland Barthes, and Charles Sanders Peirce is well documented. A succinct way of explaining these writers is really not possible, and I invite you to read them and others for yourself. However, for my purposes, I want to introduce the idea of the sign, signifier, and signified, noting simultaneously their relatedness and importance to hip hop dance, but using them in the context of an African American interpretation. These function in a system of content, form, concept, culture, and history which are shared through agreement that can almost make the system seem natural to African Americans. More will be covered on this topic later in the text when I talk about hip hop dance Signifyin' or pointing to something else, while Signification is the process of doing that within given contextual and historical frameworks.

6. Susan Foster (1995) discusses choreographed history. I am using her theory to suggest that Ebonics choreographs written history even though, at this point in time, it has been recognized only as a spoken language. I will have more to say on this point as I progress through the book.

7. Dance history and theory scholars start with the premise that dance has been categorized as ephemeral and intangible, appealing to the feminine. If you are interested in this, begin with reading Janet Wolff's *Resident Alien: Feminist Cultural Criticism* (1995) and other texts by dance theorist scholars.

8. Here is a short list of works taking up the subject of African American dance. Lynne Fauley Emery's 1972 book *Black Dance in the United States from 1619 to 1970* accurately documents dances ranging from plantation dances to contemporary black concert dance. Then there is *Stepping on the Blues: The Visible Rhythms of African American Dance* by Jacqui Malone published in 1996. And not forgetting *Jookin': The Rise of Social Dance Formations in African American Culture* written in 1990 by Katrina Hazzard-Gordon. *Negro Dance in America: A Revelation* was written as a master's thesis by Greta Griffith Brown in 1971. In 2001 a collection of essays was edited by Thomas DeFrantz entitled *Dancing Many Drums: Excavations in African American Dance.*

Nelson George *et al* wrote *Fresh; Hip Hop Don't Stop,* which gives an excellent account of breakdancing and its inception. On the black feminist side, Gwendolyn D. Pough's *Check it While I Wreck it: Black Womanhood, Hip Hop Culture, and the Public Sphere* (2004) provided a view of African American feminism in relation to hip hop music and rap, and the associations between African American female rap artistry and messages of capitalism and patriarchy. Other books about rap music, for example, Tricia Rose's *Black Noise* in 1994 or Adam Krims' *Rap Music and the Poetics of Identity* in 2000 mention aspects of breakdancing but do not spend much direct time, relative to their volume of work, on the actual subject of hip hop or African American social dance. That would make sense due to the fact that their books, extremely important and critical for us, are about rap music.

9. Kristeva (1980) provided a graphical relationship between interactions of texts such that there is a connection between them. In addition, that author noted that one must be able to read the codes of the texts in order to understand the connections and relations.

10. Richard Schechner's theory (1985) is that performance not done as practitioner is restored behavior.

PART I

HIP HOP INNOVATION

1

Theorizing Hip Hop Dance

"Dance is about saying something. If you ain't got nothin to say, get off the dance floor."
—La Vaughn Robinson, June 22, 2002
Plenary Session of the Society
of Dance History Scholars,
Philadelphia, Pennsylvania.

At first, the hip hop dance idea was ridiculed and seen as just another dance form from black folks acting the fool. It was difficult to recognize hip hop dance as text because it was discounted. A strange phenomenon materialized: hip hop dance spread 'round the globe. As such it was embraced by popular cultures from The Netherlands to Australia. Big corporations utilized it for capital gain by associating it with product and service consumption. Why did commercialization of hip hop dance work? What meanings and messages are held within it? What does codification of hip hop dance look like?

These and other questions compelled exploration into how commoditization, codification, and global capitalism in the mainstream eliminated particular theories and histories intimately woven in the original texts of hip hop dance. One consideration was that separation of the dance from its theory and history via commoditization, codification, and the effects of global capitalism denied the urgency of African Americans' outrage at their unending marginalization. This historical marginalization, it could be argued, is the social fabric the dance form emerged from, and to a large extent is what the dance speaks and writes about.

This chapter then, accomplishes several different tasks. First it reviews, for purposes of this book, relevant theoretical approaches to situate hip hop dance to ultimately answer some of these questions and necessarily raise others. Theoretical approaches include some of those used in dance theory, African American semiotics, and political economy. The reason for doing this is to build the base on which certain hip hop dances will be theorized, both in this chapter and in subsequent ones. As theory is defined by hip hop dance on the pages here, interpretations and meanings are offered. These meanings and interpretations are carried into the subsequent chapters as well. As stated before, but which will not be stated again, this is not to suggest that what is presented here is the absolute truth, the natural facts without any other interpretation. It is what this historian reads, given the experiences of this body.

Dance Theory

Dance is frequently interpreted as a momentary passing or fleeting expression that provides temporary relief from what ails you. Such a remedy when positioned this way cannot be predicted and happens only by chance. Sometimes this does happen, especially when the dancing takes place in a social setting. But those interpretations are not exclusive and exhaustive especially when we look at the text and social history embodied in hip hop as a black social dance. Writing and theorizing about hip hop dance as social history can keep hip hop dance tied to its texts, meanings and historical archives. That is the overriding purpose of this book.

Hip hop dance functions as a text and serves as public discourse not only for African Americans but for many other consumers and readers of this rich and powerful text. Hip hop as a black social dance offers texts that deliver tactical ways of being in the world as well as metaphors and theories about the world of the dancers collectively and individually. It is writing that travels not on paper but on bodies.

1. Theorizing Hip Hop Dance

This ideology is supported by work done by Susan Foster (1995). Foster pioneered choreographies of writing theory. She theorized that a body is a writing related to other bodies. In other words, no body moves or writes in isolation and dance is writing and writing is dance. Once moved, the body is never the same, and it leaves only marks and metaphors and meanings when it does move. These marks are equal to words. Foster assists readers of danced texts to answer a fundamental question: How can you find what writings a body has left? Her response to this is multifaceted.

First you have to say what bodies you are talking about. Black, white, or what have you, male or female. Then you have to define their routine activities, no matter how trivial or important, no matter what they may be. Next one must look at the collective politics pressing on the bodies. After completing the definition of the body and what it is doing, look at the assumptions others have for that body and the way the writing body says something different depending on circumstances and contexts. Now one can imagine a very black body, with lean limbs, wearing sneakers and sweats. Earrings, gold chains and if the body is male, a do-rag; if the body is female, braids with extensions. For each gender, the colors of the outfits Signify. That body is read one way. Now if the only thing that changes between these two bodies is the color of the skin, from a very black shade to one of maybe the color of coffee with a lot of cream, the bodies Signify something else. It could be that the wealthy reader sees nothing but black people entertaining them. Black people could see classism circulating throughout the African American sector of society. And the readings could be interpreted differently by the genders, in each of the groups just mentioned. But it is this that Foster is pointing to when she suggests that a body's definition and the context it finds it in writes texts for readers. Along with being read by a certain set of contextual meanings, the body reading and writing changes over time.

In regard to writing history, Foster continues, there are varied reasons for studying bodies from the past. This is accomplished through analysis of documents left behind for different reasons. The selection of documents in the writing of history is dependent on the body inhabited by the historian along with the interaction between the historian and the bodies she is writing about. The interpretation of bodies and their cultural production of meaning holds a significant key.

This goes to the notion of the cultural production of meaning, and history, and how these are interpreted. Again, relying on Foster's work, writing bodies have the same textual capabilities as the word, only accessible through understanding the interpretation of those cultural meanings. In other words, a white woman writing and studying hip hop dance history will have a different interpretation than a black woman, and each of those will in turn be different depending on their economic class, and whether they are gay or straight, for example. The same kinds of demarcations can be made for men who would write history and dance. Once these different aspects of the body are integrated, then we can have choreographed historical writing.

Taking a panoptic view of the areas of bodily writing and scholarly research from different fields, Foster concluded that choreographers, dance notation scholars, and anthropologists developed a categorical and anatomical analysis of the body, fueling the notion of dance as a natural phenomenon. She indicated that it was as late as the 1960s when Foucault and Barthes theoretical approaches emerged that the body became non-natural, a "relation between signifier and signified" (Foster 1995, 14). Between that period and her publication she argued that dance studies had not given the body agency either because the field neglected "choreographic intent" (Foster 1995, 15). Doing so, however, positions dance as a body writing and allows dance making to be a form of theorizing. She writes, "Where bodily endeavors assume the status of forms of articulation and representation, their movements acquire a status and function equal to the words that describe them" (Foster 1995, 9). This is one of the aspects of theorizing that forms a foundation for understanding messages and meanings in hip hop dance. The form is chronologically charged, loaded, weighted, interpretable, and deep with meaning and understanding of what being black involves, of what being a black man involves, and of what being a black woman involves.

My writing here on these pages as an African American dance historian and marketing professor necessarily means that I view the world as an African American woman and will record what I observe in a manner that reflects my positionality within the world. Furthermore, my writing here on these pages depends, as Foster says, on the protective covering given to me through corporeal meanings embedded in my physical practices derived from my identification with African American experiences. The same can be said of African American hip hop dance historians, whom we customarily recognize as dancers recording observations that are embedded in bodily corporeal meanings stemming from their experiences in America. The method of documentation is based on, and at the same time protected by, their positionality within the world. Going further, Foster makes statements that I must quote at length here, which stage the way body-history writing and research take place:

> To choreograph history, then, is first to grant that history is made by bodies, and then to acknowledge that all those bodies, in moving and documenting their movements, in learning about past movement, continually conspire together and are conspired against.... These past and present bodies transit to a mutually constructed semiosis. Together they configure a tradition of codes and conventions of bodily signification that allows bodies to represent and communicate with other bodies. Together they put pen to page. Together they dance with words [Foster 1995, 10–11].

Seen and understood this way, we can return agency and give credibility to African American hip hop dancing bodies — pull the rug right out from underneath ideologies that push hip hop dance as a mere commercial-popular-culture-young-people's-profit maximizing thing.

Along with Foster's theoretical approach to writing, it will be necessary to undermine essentializing black people and hip hop dance since it is not because black people are black that we dance, that we like dancing, or that we can.[1] A feminist analysis provided by Foster in a later work (1998) will be helpful in achieving this aim. Following Teresa de Lauretis' (1990) theorization of essentializing, Foster set forth an expanded view of gender such that it extends beyond biological aspects.

According to Foster, the mental habit of essentializing involves ways of interpreting. It is what people do to simplify, avoid, live in denial and form procedures for purchasing goods and services. Only there it is referred to perhaps as a heuristic. When it mutates into essentials, so to speak, we say the Chinese people are good at so and so even if they have tight eyes, or the Germans are terrific at producing automobiles even if they have that history hanging over their heads from the Nazis, or the Americans do not produce but those black Americans sure can work (produce) and dance. Such habits of mind, or attitudes as they can be called, extend to gender, race, dance, and the ways in which theories are applied in the field of cultural studies. Foster deconstructed this stance as it relates to gender and used dance as her medium. To accomplish this, she established that a separation was needed to show how one has to think through relationships between, for example, performance and theory. She argued that dance is the performance (a skill), and choreography is the text (theory). By extension therefore, black people can both dance (a skill) and choreograph (write theory).

To make her point, Foster described a general creative process embarked upon by choreographers, and choreographers' assignments of responsibilities to bodies. The assignments both are gender- and ethno-dependent. Once choreography is written it is adapted and changed deliberately or not (improvisation is how one may think of this) by dancers who will perform it. Uppermost in the mind though is that the improvisations do not eliminate the choreographic intent. Over time, a choreographic score complete with improvisational performance becomes accessible to viewers. It is clear that anything but a natural phenomenon has occurred during this creative process, and this kind of process occurs with the black social dance called hip hop.

Foster then turned to break dancing, relying on Banes (1981) and Rose (1994) to support the argument that social change, relations between men and women, dance, and time are interwoven. (Banes' analysis of break dancing was descriptive, whereas Rose's is theoretical, separate treatments of the skill versus theory dichotomy.) In the break dancing scenario, black males choreographed historical texts reflecting political concerns while later, black women choreographed in support of the black males' agenda while simultaneously creating their own feminism. Foster concluded that choreography and systems of representation (theories), mixed with the skill to execute and improvise the dance, yielded the "cultural moment" wherein hip hop dance could be read. This, as it is understood and used in the context of hip hop dance, forms the nexus that erases the habit of essentializing. In other words, hip hop dance is not a naturally black thang but came to pass as a result of certain processes. Those processes included body writing about socioeconomics and politics, reading the reflections and projections of images of people on and off of each other, and documents of historical interactions.

Methods for reading dance have come not only from dance theories, but also from ethnography. Adrienne Kaeppler (1972) argued that dance ethnology was descriptive, second order, and meaningful only if the descriptive data were analyzed using ethnographic theory and method. Expanding the ways in which dance was studied in the field, she used an ethno-scientific approach so that the resulting description would be equal to learning to speak a language, giving "a reader the information necessary to operate as a member of the society" (Kaeppler 1972, 173). Simultaneously, one had to determine which movements, movements that in her view were likened to linguistics, were important to the members of society and which ones were not, whether they were *emic* or *etic*. In her view, "*emic*" equaled differences recognized in movements by a particular culture, whereas *etic* represented differences in movement that were considered culture-free. Kaeppler then moved into setting up a general method for learning and analyzing dances from producers of a particular dance tradition.

Using this point of view it could be argued that hip hop dance was first order, given in an *emic* framework. African Americans knew how to operate in a society that was fraught with double meanings and Signfications but nevertheless could write documents with their bodies using a language that was accessible to those who spoke it. Interpretations provided daily ways of being, knowledge of what to do, and theories about the world. It could be argued, then, that hip hop dance *etic* emerged later yielding a dance that Others copied for entertainment value only. Then it re-emerged as an *emic* within societies under the pressure of capitalism and globalization, as an *emic* for articulating issues.

Historically, other assumptions were made about dance, in addition to the notion that dance is non-theoretical, and can only be described. That dance is feminine, freeing, intuitive, and non-verbal has anchored and bounded it away from theoretical models for centuries. Janet Wolff (1995) examined this; she insisted that dance required cultural analysis. Moreover, she brought to light, in her critique of feminist theory and dance, that dance as "freeing" had only been subject to women dancers. In this association, dance was seen as intuitive, natural, and non-verbal by virtue of its being separated from the male, which was considered verbal. Instead of seeing dance this way, she argued that dance could never be separated or occur outside of language because talking and dancing work and create together. When teaching, choreographing, or performing, Wolff noted that stories were being told with bodies, written program notes were often available for concert dances, and sometimes words were incorporated into the performance. "The experience of dance, by its performers or by its audiences, can never be an experience outside language" (Wolff 1995, 80). At the same time, Wolff believed as Foster suggested, that dance is mediated by culture and is a social practice. As an aside, I may add that men's dance does not equate to freedom but rather something else. Wolff never really said what men's dance is. In the hip hop dance world these separations did not occur however. Separation of the dance in its entirety did though as evidenced by the plethora of male rappers, violence, books, articles, and analysis of hip hop music (the masculine) and little on hip hop dance (the feminine).

At this point then a summary may be organizing. First we have hip hop dance as a creative text written in relation to the body's placement on the planet, interpreted by readers. Hip hop dance is written about depending on the body doing the writing. Hip hop dance not being an essential function of black people, not being natural, not being feminine. The dance could be considered an emic expression useful as an *etic* and then reforming as an *emic* again. Because it gives a way to interpret, theorize, and tactically negotiate life, it is not to be understood as a writing that can cure ailments or be disregarded as a feminine unimportant endeavor. It is language, it is a system of Signification and has meaning. Now that this picture has been sketched and this foundation placed, it would be useful to consider some work that has been done in African and African American studies as it relates to hip hop dance.

Hip Hop Dance and African American Language

June Jordan wrote about ways black people communicate (1988). In one of her essays in *On Call*, she described the differences between Black English and Standard White (American) English, and went so far as to show the rules of the language, verb system, tenses and so forth, and how these are different than that of Standard White English. Moreover, Jordan gave the reader background explaining the lengths that black people have gone to distance themselves from the notion of the wrongness of Black English, and how that language has not been given legitimacy in written form. As such, she indicated that Black English could be viewed as an "endangered species, as a perishing, irreplaceable system of community intelligence, or we should expect its extinction, and along with that, the extinguishing of much that constitutes our own proud, and singular identity" (1988, 123). This is contrary to the ways in which Black English has been used in mainstream media and advertising placements, the ways in which certain phrases have been adapted into what we know as American English such that it is "becoming more Black, or less White, despite the expected homogenizing effects of television, and other mass media" (Jordan 1988, 124).

And unlike Standard American English writing and speaking, there are three aspects to Black English that set it apart from the usual ways in which we think about language structure. Black English, written or spoken, is linked, as Jordan relates, to an existential phenomenon.[2] It is not a "death of the author" approach as suggested by Foucault and Barthes.[3] Rather, Black English is comprised of "life, voice, and clarity" which takes place in the present tense. Indeed, she points out this clear distinction between Standard American English and Black English:

> Our [Black] language evolves from a culture that abhors all abstraction, or anything tending to obscure or delete the fact of the human being who is here and now/the truth of the person who is speaking or listening.... Every sentence assumes the living and active participation of at least two human beings, the speaker and the listener [Jordan 1988, 129].

Black English as Jordan spoke of is what I define as US Ebonics (Ebonics from now on) for purposes of this book. Ebonics mainly functions as an oral communication method, structured and varied, but constantly evolving in its intricacies.

I concur and extend Jordan's interpretation of Black English as a way of understanding hip hop dance as another means of non-written communication. The dance represents the desire to "say something real to somebody real" (Jordan 1988, 129). At issue here is the notion that hip hop dance speaks not in a language that would be recognizable as white, but rather in a language that is inherently black, one that exists, one that developed parallel to, and in opposition to, an existing domination to give the speaker presence and life rather than absence and death. It would be a supposition therefore that other dances also speak in a particular language for particular reasons.

Tricia Rose pushed this ideology further in *Black Noise* (1994). Rose's work primarily focused on a history of rap music as it was situated within a broader context of hip hop culture, which she defines as comprising lyrics, dance, and graffiti coming into being during the late 1970s.[4] Note that within the structure of hip hop, each of their aspects represents what we could consider the male and female roles of communication, i.e., male writing and speaking, and female movement. However, it would do well to suggest that these taxonomies are useful only in helping us to categorize aspects of hip hop. All of them are methods of communicating which use Signification and Signifying and until subjected to media and commercialization, defied the taxonomic structure.

Gates' (1988) work, as mentioned in the Preface, is far and away the most substantially applicable explanation of the complexity involved in communicating through Ebonics that underlies hip hop — dance, lyrics, and writing. The fact of the matter is that African Americans appropriated and continue to appropriate for their own use, for the distraction of non-fluent readers and the informing of the fluent ones, a completely new system of communicating. The new system is as distorted as a hall of mirrors, Gates says, in trying to comprehend the ways in which "identical signifiers" and homonyms form the basis of simultaneous trickery and knowingness (Gates 1988, 45). Moreover and significantly, "The relationship that black 'Signification' bears to the English 'signification' is, paradoxically, a relation of difference inscribed within a relation of identity" which, together with Signifying creates "a noisy disturbance in silence" (Gates 1988, 45). In other words, this becomes yet another method used in acquiring a systematic communication mechanism functioning outside the boundaries of domination: We got our own thang we got yours and you ain't got ours.

Like Jordan by implication (1988) and Gates overtly (1988), Rose (1994) suggested that the principles underlying hip hop provided a "blueprint for social resistance and affirmation" (Rose 1994, 39). Employing a critical theorist approach par excellence, she surmised that the lyrics arose and gave way to social rupture, lyrics which themselves are written in Ebonics. So it is with the dance. That is to say, the language of hip hop dance layers, embellishes, resists (Rose 1994, 39), but further it comments, teaches, warns, and transforms messages and meanings into readable commentaries. Such commentaries can be social ruptures, but they can also be historical, theoretical, strategic, and tactical texts. Much like a mathematical proof, the texts can build upon themselves, arriving at the answer if you will, only after conducting a series of required steps which have to be performed before the answer has meaning.

Thomas De Frantz's *The Black Beat Made Visible: Hip Hop Dance and Body Power* (2004) supports the notions that hip hop dance speaks, and has dual communication modes that are comprised of powerful building blocks resulting in "corporeal orature" (De Frantz 2004, 67). Moreover, he believed that the corporeal orature resides within the African American domain: if you are outside of it something is lost in translation. Therefore De Frantz is saying, as is the mathematical formula done correctly, that not only do black people have the ability to create outside the existing channels using a methodological approach, but also that their creative methods yield power to act, an answer to something, a theory, a proof.[5]

Knowing these theoretical foundations for hip hop dance, what then can be said about projecting the dance onto the screen? What happens to it when it is taken from the empowering structure that it is to an image in advertising? While this topic will be covered extensively in the chapter on hip hop dance and commercialization, it is useful to discuss what goes on from the point of view of what can be called theoretical undermining — that is when the dance is used outside the contexts within which it was created.

Hip Hop Dance and Social Identity

Allowing the dance to Signify and theorize at the level of the individual raises the issue of what type of social, or more macro, texts exist when certain phrases are connected with others and particularly over time. We know from the above paragraphs that the work done by this dance form is done with the expectation of presence. Does it also then allow for documentation as a primary text, a selected volume of history or historicizing?

Jane C. Desmond took this to task in her essay "Embodying Difference" found in *Meaning in Motion* (1997). She raised a number of interesting points, some of which will be useful in the analysis of hip hop dance texts. First she indicated that by studying dance texts, increased understanding of social identity, along with its negotiation, geographic and historical contexts can be achieved. Next she addressed the ways in which dance texts shift meanings when the text migrates from one group to another. Specifically, movement styles are "an important mode of distinction between social groups and it is usually actively learned or passively absorbed in the home and community ... a primary text ... that signals group affiliation and group differences" (1997, 31) that make sense only in context with other people.

1. Theorizing Hip Hop Dance

Recognition of movement as a primary social text can be had by those who can write it and read it. By this framework Desmond's analysis indicated that there is an *emic* and *etic* classification system, in that some dances are appropriate and necessary if danced by certain individuals while at the same time the awareness of who is not dancing which dance is germane (1997, 32). The ability to notice these sets of distinction further allows reading of class and economic status. These readings then constitute attitudes that are used in assessing bodies. And more, by being able to trace these historical attitudes of assessment, we can see changes in social fabrics of one group reading dance to another.

Following upon this argument, hip hop dance needs to be understood and elevated to primary contextual social text. It further needs analysis as a migratory text that moved from one social group, if you will, to another under *emic* and *etic* circumstances. Going from black to white; having black mean one thing at one time, and having it mean something else at a later time. Having hip hop dance traced back to the African Diaspora and Middle Passage to slavery, through all the trials and tribulations of freedom, segregation, affirmative action, and globalization. The reader may recall that for long periods of time, which time can include the present moment, some groups saw it as a travesty to be black. Few wanted to drink water after a black person or get into a pool if a black person had been in it before them. You know the issues that are being referenced here and there is no need for a complete restatement of them. However, those beliefs were not limited to groups in the United States, but rather circulated throughout the world in other areas where slave trades and colonization took place. Then being black became, during the 1970s, something else. It was still a tragedy to be black but it was affirmed. More will be said about the economics of this period of time which was extremely instrumental in developing hip hop dance. For now though, with the circulation of *etic* hip hop dance images through global media, what does it mean now to be black? How does this *etic* form a new *emic,* or does it?

Referring again to Desmond, she suggested that dance texts mutate but retain traces of their origin even while being "refashioned" for new and different purposes (1997, 37). That point being made, a main purpose that is now beneficial to contemplate and consider is that hip hop dance texts as *emic* facilitated creation of and circulated in many imagined communities, such communities as described by Benedict Anderson (1983). Anderson's work traced the ways in which people developed mental connections and affiliations with one another in disparate geographies comprising real or non-real (imaginary) nations. Keep in mind that the concepts of nation and nationalism are constructions that have meaning only within the realm of cultural artifact in that these have to exist as an agreement between members of a society. Moreover, these concepts and constructions are invented and endure for particular purposes.

Further, Anderson demonstrated that these mental connections have been formed, and broken, and reformed at the pleasure of the dominant during different political and economic regimes, at different points in time. The mental connections to polities are and were facilitated, and in fact formulated, by language, religion, and capitalism along with all of the underlying cultural and social controls embedded in each of these institutions. At its core, imagined communities involve a Marxist point of view concerning the segmentation of people into two main world-classes *vis a vis* relations to production, that is, the proletariat and the bourgeoisie (Anderson 1983, 4).

The imagined community has several different underlying principles that must be kept in mind, but only a few of them will be addressed here.[6] "It is *imagined* because the members of even the smallest nation will never know most of their fellow-members, meet them, or even hear of them, yet in the minds of each lives the image of their communion" (Anderson 1983, 6, italics original). And while imagined, the nation or community comprises millions, even billions of people, infiltrating it with finiteness rather than a construction that is boundless. Comprised of people who work hard and capitalists who extract the surplus value of the labor "it is imagined as a *community*, because, regardless of the actual inequality and exploitation that may prevail in each, the nation is always conceived as a deep, horizontal comradeship. Ultimately it is a fraternity that makes it possible, over the past two centuries, for so many millions of people, not so much to kill, as willingly to die for such limited imaginings" (Anderson, 1983, 7, italics original). And it is time bound, so that each person within the imagined community has a sense of urgency, a relational commitment to doing something while others are, or an understanding that others have done something, have endured something. Anderson suggested that one can think of this simultaneous consumption as it was done with newspapers, which he suggested was a fictional depiction of what was actually taking place in a geographic location.

For purposes of hip hop dance texts, the nation of dancers in the global imagined community has expanded resulting from increased segmentation and segregation as capital seeks its highest returns. However, the real community of black people has had direct experience with the effects of capital flows and as such know how to do something, have endured dealing with it. Now though the communication device that had been used to theorize and teach has been appropriated showing not the pain of the past but the fictional happiness of the present. This image is circulated to show that hard work eventually pays off. Now black people they got game, got bank, and got it goin' on, even though at one time they was slaves, but don't go there. What better image of consumption and success to project? Now the imagined community of people who are next to homeless (this includes marginalized whites, laborers in corporate America, and so on, in the hip hop dance nation) but pretend that they are not, comprises the worldwide consumption machine contributing to the world-class dichotomy which is a truly American phenomenon, a fiction that promises prosperity with hard work linked to hip hop dance. Consumption is a cool thing, and without our direct knowing, is the only way the world continues to turn — profits. Those profits are not had without a level of state intervention so that the flow of capital seeks the highest profit, coming from the touch of that shipment, with that product, with those peoples, married in this fashion, administered by those governments, during that time (Anderson 1983, 63, 115). Hip hop dance has now become the unofficial language of the state to coerce profit making. Indeed, as Scott remarked hip hop dance "has been claimed as American culture's true indigenous dance expression, but not officially....

The pressure of global capital on the local site of creation and performance renders the act of creation into the repetition of production" (Scott
2001, 107, 127). And some would have us believe that the unofficial language is a natural occurrence among peoples within an imagined community, oppressed and simultaneously ready to die for new kitchen
appliances, automobiles, and fashion furniture paid for with no interest or payments for twelve months?[7]

Not only do imagined communities inform the text. Hip hop
dance speaks to a global nation of real laborers of multiple ethnicities,
trying to imagine their lives worth living under capitalist economics.
What better image to use than hip hop dance texts as *etic*? Emmanuel
Wallerstein's *Geopolitics and Geocultures* (1992) and his earlier *The Capitalist World-Economy* (1979) critically examine the fate of laborers,
states and polities, economic systems, and corporations using a historical Marxist interpretation. Each page of his work is thick with information; it feels like a treatise that was channeled from some higher
power regarding the state of capitalism that we have to look forward
to, and it is impossible to reproduce it here. Let it suffice then for it
to be said of his work that what was being drawn in his first book was
the explanation of the capitalist world economy as part of a process of
humanity moving from point A to point B as a global society, point B
being that place in which it is realized that the process of capital accumulation has been harmful. Nevertheless, the world market has to be
explored in order to arrive at point B — whatever that may be, but
assuredly it is better than capitalism. In the second publication Wallerstein suggested that even though all aspects of the ways in which capital has been extracted runs against an individual's sense of self
preservation it remains part of this process and this is the reason people do it. The process of going from this point to that future point
involves the production and manufacture of cultural structure at the
world level (1992, 169). That cultural structure affords the working
body an imagined community engaged in economically controlling
devices at the individual level, such as the African Diaspora and slavery, sexism, and unequal wealth distribution (1992, 169). Focusing on
the function of racism as such a device, Wallerstein supposed that we

have now moved from one of the capitalist world economy's control mechanisms to a new one: race consciousness. Race consciousness (you know: a politically correct and sometimes not really believed national view that the way in which the dominant class treated those people was wrong) grew out of racism and in so doing linked some sort of positive nationalism with a trope that had previously been negative. Now by inference, race consciousness has infiltrated hip hop dance texts, facilitating the imagined communities, furthering both consumption and exploitation on the one hand and profit maximization on the other. Adopt hip hop dance as the universal dance language and you too can overcome. It is a response, a textual response, to and a theorization of certain social issues. These include, but are not limited to, institutionalized global capitalism, racism, and race consciousness. Ellen Graff described a similar local phenomenon in *Stepping Left* (1997). Writing about dance texts in the 1930s and 1940s during a particularly turbulent social and economic period, she believed people were "driven by a kind of moral fervor to respond to the complex social and political issues surrounding them" (Graff 1997, 3). There was and is a moral fervor to the pitch and pace of profit taking around the globe, at the juncture of creation and circulation of hip hop dance. Of course, it is not to suggest that people will dance to fix what ails them. However, believe that some black people have qualifications to talk to working bodies and help them with the theorization process. How that gets manipulated is up to the capitalist world economic engine.

At the same time, hip hop dance as text facilitates profit production via multiculturalism through corporatism. In terms of multiculturalism, the reference is made to the deliberate production of a sense of community designed by the corporation to foster reaping of profits from working bodies. Multiculturalism as presented and used here is not an ephemeral natural melding of a fantasy of "we are the world" and living in paradise because we all get along. No, it is not that. It is the dissemination of images to imagined communities that serve to keep the working classes working and the wealthy class wealthy. Producing multiculturalism with the purpose of commodification is concerned with corporate interests, not individual interests. Anything that can be usurped will be used to achieve this end, including "cultural difference separated out from the material conflicts" of the community in which they arose (Lowe 1997, 87). Hip hop dance is used for those same reasons, that is, in the production of multiculturalism for ends pursued by profit seekers.

And it may be useful to think about what a global corporation is, and while raising questions ask exactly what is corporatism? Corporations can be multinational, national, or global depending on the ways in which products or services are produced, and the ways in which the product or service is marketed. A national corporation sees itself as being bound with the geographic borders of the nation in which it resides, and uses only a set of domestic marketing strategies. Notice that a national company can be American but be located elsewhere. A multinational corporation sees itself as using multiple marketing strategies to fit different geographies around the globe, where as a global company markets it products and services as if it has only one market.[8] Corporatism, according to Merriam Webster "is the organization of a society into industrial and professional corporations serving as organs of political representation and exercising some control over persons and activities within their jurisdiction" (www.m-w.com). Note that the corporation itself is seen, in this and other legal definitions, as an organism, an entity of its own body, soul, mind, and spirit, but no one person is responsible for it.

But these definitions and approaches to the corporation, while themselves slippery and complex enough, exclude other aspects of globalization necessary to situate the ways in which hip hop dance functions within it. Consider what Fredric Jameson (1998) theorized about globalization. He believed that "globalization is a communicational concept, which alternately masks and transmits cultural or economic meanings" (Jameson 1998, 55). These meanings can have positive or negative connotations, depending on how they are read and interpreted. On the one hand it can mean the celebration of difference while on the other it cataclysmically forces "rapid assimilation of hitherto autonomous markets [to support] forced integration of countries all over the globe into precisely that new global division of labor ... a picture of standardization on an unparalleled new scale ... integration into a system from which 'delinking' is unthinkable and inconceivable" (1998, 57). With this combined celebration and forced standardization we have a colonization that is unprecedented. People watch it on TV, produce it for Wal-Mart.

I posit that this hip hop dance as an *emic* text is written and embodied through hip hop dance *etic* that is separated from its citational contexts by transnational and multinational corporations' assertion and sale of the thrill of multiculturalism to oppressed ethnic groups. Unreferenced and plagiarized, and aside from the negative images of blacks paraded across television and movie screens, commoditized hip hop dance texts say to people of different cultures, via consumption seduction, they should remain contented and get along with each other.[9] But the fact of the matter is the capitalists want consuming submissive labor so that their profits remain stable or better yet increase, and this cannot happen if laborers do not get along.

Transnational and multinational corporations advocate multiculturalism and simultaneously press for a global culture of consumerism and materialism. Three types of dances (which will be explained in a moment), waack, break dancing and rap dance texts — originally social commentary texts about life as African Americans and a communicative theoretical text between African Americans — are now detached from their references and appropriated into mass media, furthering a separation of profit maximizers and global laborers. The separation is achieved by directing the gaze of laborers through the media, so we focus on consumption rather than social, economic and political equality. The effect of directed gazing prevents sustained and real change in the economic and racial situations ethnic groups find themselves in. In a subsequent chapter some statistics are provided that explain what the directed gaze distracts us from.

For now though, let it suffice to say that the fact of the matter is that uncontextualized hip hop dance text sells anything it is associated with, even an imagined community. It is really common to find television commercials using hip hop dance to sell products and services. As a researcher that studies consumer behavior, I have watched and analyzed many commercials that use hip hop dance in its allure, product positioning, and consumption promise based on the commercial's intended target markets. A few are offered here.

It would be instrumental to show photo stills of commercials and popular films depicting the *etic* of hip hop dance. Unfortunately, using photo stills, that is, gaining proper and legal permission, is difficult. In contacting the corporations and asking permission to use such stills, much resistance arose. For the most part, the corporations will not agree to the use of their photographs if they do not agree with the analysis of the photograph or the context in which it is placed in a publication. Film producers will not agree to a complementary use; most often they ask for thousands of dollars for a few reproductions. With regard to the corporate policy this is due to the fact that any popular or massive knowledge of the manipulation will undermine the whole construction and invalidate the *etic* of the text. In regard to the film makers, what we have is the same end result, but formulated only as a monetary barrier. Therefore, within this book, summaries of selected commercials and film scenes have to suffice. The reader may check online to find these ads or view short clips of the films by using a search engine and entering a few appropriate key words.

For example, JC Penney used hip hop dance choreography with children during back-to-school advertising periods in August and September. The girls in the ads were doing hip hop dances like The Runnin Man, standing like they were hip hop dance gangsters, holding the hip hop dance attitude. Quaker Oats Cereal used hip hop dance to push its product by showing a black family eating oatmeal on a large turntable dancing The Runnin Man to a scratched beat. Dog food producers for Kibbles and Bits designed commercials utilizing computer graphics to show a dog doing a hip hop dance, The Cabbage Patch, because of the dog's happiness with the flavor and substance of the food. Jell-O Pudding used hip hop dance, this time The Snake, placed on a dancing cow and a little boy to talk about the wiggle of the pudding and how cool it is to eat it, internalize it. Pepto-Bismol used several of the dances placed on many bodies to convince you that hip hop dance is the solution to your digestive problems. And this is only a short list of the sites of *etic* representations of hip hop dance, fueling consumption, taken out of context.

In this section it was shown that hip hop dance started as a primary text, and functioned as an *emic* when written and read within historical social contexts. Because of that it functioned as a source of identification. Importantly, discussion of the *emic* and *etic* texts as underlying constructions of imagined community was brought forth. While the dance may have been taken for use in pushing products, it could also be argued that the messages and meanings in the dance form allowed the growing world class of laborers, under a most clandestine and pathetic colonialism, to understand their predicament, following on the knowledge produced by the historical texts written by African Americans. Hip hop dance has become the official language by which products and services gets produced, and simultaneously, consumption is made to appear natural. The entire process produces a mesmerized individual.

Hip Hop Dance as Text—Three in Search of Meaning

Katrina Hazzard-Donald does an excellent job of listing, categorizing and documenting hip hop dance. In *Droppin' Science: Critical Essays on Rap Music and Hip Hop Culture* (1996), she provided a brief history of hip hop music and dance. Her essay entitled "Dance in Hip Hop Culture" gave readers a great deal of information. It included hip hop's historical influences from slavery, its African ancestry, and American social and economic influences on African Americans reflected by and in hip hop dance. In that work, she traced three phases of hip hop dance connected to this rich background and history. She labeled these phases as waack, break dancing, and rap dance.

Waack, the earliest form of hip hop dance developed in 1972. Within the waack phase, Hazzard-Donald referenced dances like Locking, The Robot and The Spank, as well as moves like splits, spins and freezes. Many of these texts were written by male dancers. Splits, spins, and freezes provided punctuation in many cases, to phrases written that contained Locking, The Robot, and The Spank. Waack provides, in my view, a theorem that was used like a building block, having been built upon, to bring hip hop dance to its next phase, break dancing.

Break dancing itself was competitive but most often performed by African American men. Break dancing has been likened to a physical form of playing-the-dozens in African American communities, where Signification and Signifyin are taken to a most elevated and intellectual level. Simply stated, in the danced text, the men competed with each other through dance moves that outperformed challengers in the physical conversation, which is similar to what they do in the verbal dozens, where men compete with each other in making verbal commentary. Women played the dozens as well and participated in writing the texts associated with break dancing.

Participants in the verbal form of the game have to be quick witted in order to be successful. Break dancing too involves a quickwit of sorts — but on a physical level. The dance utilizes acrobatics, head spins, backspins, and Moon Walking, which are not moves for the stiff, slow witted or slow bodied. These two phases of hip hop dance, waack and break dancing, were performed on public stages with no proscenium, such as in parks or on street corners, and were popular from 1972 through 1974. It did not take long for break dancing to draw popular attention. Hazzard-Donald places break dancing's appearance in the mass media in April 1981, which she pointed out marked the beginning of the decline of the dance's competitiveness. Stated differently, it marked the movement from one group to another, the shift from *emic* to *etic* and also marked hip hop dance's rise in commoditization and codification.

Rap dance, which is where the main focus of this work will center, grew out of waack and break dancing, combines house dance (dance done in clubs and at house parties) in its performance. The advent of rap dance is where the supposedly predominantly male performance characteristic of waack and break dance shifted to include women. There is no doubt however, from this researcher's experience, that both dance texts included women, but the male writers were the ones gaining the attention. The dances were not couples dances but they were danced by both genders. In any event, as with break dance and waack,

Hazzard-Donald related, rap dance was not considered a couples dance. Rather, rap dance included The Roger Rabbit, house dancing, and The Runnin Man, all of which have been demonstrated in professionally choreographed performances. Indeed, choreographed rap dance occurs in the *etic* of the mass media's handiwork, as for example in a recent TV commercial I saw that depicted a white man doing The Runnin Man to sell computer business solutions. In order to expand its scope there are two other dances that I add to this list of rap dances identified by Hazzard-Donald. They are The Cabbage Patch and The Snake (1980's version). Of course, there are hundreds of rap dances, too many to catalog for this particular volume of work. For ease of writing, I will from now on refer to hip hop dance as a collective text, and specify only the three categories within the text, i.e., breaking, waack, and rap dance, when it will add clarity to the interpretive meanings.

The economic and political state of affairs in this country affects African Americans. Poverty, unemployment, and crime are reported daily and moreover are measured by the US Department of Labor. The main media attention generally focuses on the negative. Many popular culture images portray stereotypes wherein black rappers, gangsters, athletes, and entertainers are read by certain groups as dangerous or comedic. Black women are read as whores or big mamas. Both groups read as a threat of some kind, with a connection to oppression and free labor lingering in the memory. At the same time, little if any positive mainstream media attention is paid to accomplished black professionals. These observations are not new to the reader, without a doubt. What is new is the possibility that hip hop dance provides a documentary and commentary vehicle for messages and voices that are not conveyed, not considered important in the main communication devices employed by American society. Couple this non-conveyance with poverty, historically high unemployment (Mos Def, *Mathematics*, 1999), police brutality, and intra- and interracial sexism. Match these events further with the colonial history of African Americans that reinforces racism and recent decreases in affirmative action initiatives. Accomplishing all of this and other historical events too numerous to list here then achieves the development of the *emic* of hip hop dance.

The dance, along with its documentary and commentary functions, contextualizes this social history. It links backward through time at least to the Middle Passage and the African Diaspora. That reference in time is a critical one since large masses of African people were moved from their continent to others, and generally without their favorable consent, which immediately brought to bear an imagined community. Africans knew they were a part of but apart from Africa, knew that people they were related to or not had been similarly dispersed. The imagined community developed under the economic and political system, using Signified and Signifyin dance as one of its communication and writing devices. It would be beneficial at this juncture to discuss several dances related to this history, and show their linkages to today's messages. They are The Snake, The Cabbage Patch, and The Runnin Man.

The Snake shows the *emic* reader of the dance how to avoid adversity and how to appear undisturbed by it. It also instructs the reader regarding survival methods when being ambushed from all angles. When writing The Snake, the body remains essentially still, but the head and neck and upper torso engage in movement. Holding the arms out to the sides, slightly bent and at about ribcage level, the head leads the neck and shoulders to one side, returns to center, and then repeats the action to the other side. It would be as if you were told that you must remain in a given physical space, standing up. Then you are told that physical objects will be flying at, launched at, your face and shoulders. And finally, the instructions indicate that you may avoid the objects being sent your way and remain alive only by moving your body from the waist up.

Some objects are non-physical, namely adversity. We usually recognize these as statistics, some of which are described in *Street Soldier* by Joseph Marshall, Jr., and Lonnie Wheeler (1996). Marshall and Wheeler found that more young African American men are murdered each year in the US than were killed by lynching in all the years of American history. In the 1980s, drug abuse among African American children rose 150 percent. Arrests for heroin and cocaine abuse increased ten times faster for African American children than for whites. More than half of African American children live with no father, three times as many as white children. Forty-six percent of African American children live in poverty. Every eleven minutes an African American child is arrested for some violent crime, based on a stereotype. Every eleven minutes a black girl has her second, her *second*, baby. Every 69 seconds a black baby is born when the father is absent. Seventy-five percent of African American men between 25 and 34 years old who dropped out of high school are either in jail, on probation or on parole. We make up 12.4 percent of all the people in the US but comprise more than 50 percent of the prison population.

These statistics are disturbing to say the least. However hip hop dance began as a commentary on these statistics, layered upon other historical facts. Therefore another intangible object can be identified as the state of affairs facing America and the relations between whites and blacks. We have seen different attempts at erasure of the historical evidences of slavery and a blaming mechanism with respect to Africans and their arrival on this continent, a formulation of African Americans as "a people without a history" (Wolf 1997). The Snake textualizes and theorizes both the tangible and intangible, giving a way to write history, both individual and collective. Seen this way, it is quite easy to ask the following qualified rhetorical question: In the *etic* version, The Snake as shown in the Jell-O Pudding commercial, all of these meanings have been stripped away. What does eating pudding that wiggles around have to do with any of these primary textual issues?

This is a great point of departure for the next text to be read: The Cabbage Patch. It denotes happiness at attaining something long sought after, either by legitimate or illegitimate means. For example Martin Lawrence does The Cabbage Patch in the movie *Nothin' to Lose* (Touchstone 2000) after he and the protagonist successfully stole money as part of an overall revengeful plot. Another reading of celebration after attainment is shown when the animated dog on the Kibbles and Bits commercial does The Cabbage Patch after eating a satisfying bowl of dog food. Moreover, The Cabbage Patch is often danced in association with scoring in sports games and among people who win sweep-stakes. Importantly, writing The Cabbage Patch was initially about how black people could get over, historically succeeding politically, economically, socially. Linking it with consumption in the media made sense because the dance writes celebratory messages, giving support for finding ways to succeed despite an unsupportable environment, or impossible odds.

The Cabbage Patch is done by moving your upper body around in a circle. You lean back and push your arms away from you as if stirring a large pot of dough with a long wooden and heavy spoon. Every time your hands come close to your body, you push them back toward the other edge of the pot. The feet are firmly planted in parallel position, knees slightly bent, and with no readable facial affect. Some of The Cabbage Patch writers continue with the circular motions until their knees are in a squatting position. This dance, like The Snake, was normally performed at social events at someone's home.

Aside from a celebratory writing, another of the historical texts written by this dance is solidarity in or political support for African American community, a community that has been stolen and stolen from. Face the facts: mass community efforts have been undermined, from the Underground Railroad to the Million Man March; leaders have been manipulated to turn on each other and outright killed; affirmative action laws repealed; and often times hope itself was stolen. Additionally social dignity and individual self-respect have been significantly tampered with, creating a dysfunction within families and within the social fabric of American society. The desire is to find a way out of these senseless and often contrived circles, simultaneously looking for meaning and answers. Many of the statistics mentioned above, while true, need to be juxtaposed to the successes, and details of positive statistics are given in a subsequent chapter. Suffice it to say for now that we need to hear about how many blacks are doing well in their careers, those that have remained happily married, and those that have been leaders in changing history in positive, albeit small, ways. Therefore a message in The Cabbage Patch text has to be read thusly: You are stealing from us. We know it. We make it look like we are going around in circles, but in reality we Signifyin. We are slowly but surely, and quietly, getting over. The Cabbage Patch *etic* forms in its first definition mainly. Celebrate consuming something. Black people know how, so now you can too. You have earned it. By the same token, this *etic* masks the degree of the stolen surplus value taken from the working class.

The final dance for consideration in this section of the book describing rap dance is The Runnin Man. This is the only text in this category that involves movement of the arms, legs, and feet. The torso is exceptionally quiet. The dance is performed with clenched fists, a manner of running in place but with the feet sliding on the floor, reminiscent of a Michael Jackson Moon Walk. The head does not move. The arms pump up and down like you are reaching with both hands to close a stiff window that keeps springing up. The affect shows strained expression. Performing this dance one wears tennis shoes and a loose-fitting sweat-suit or workout clothes. It is done in choreographed sequences more often than for example, within social dance venues of homes and night clubs because the dance requires a considerable amount of space be given to the dancer.

What this dance signifies is running in place — working for centuries — and anger: muscle memory of anger in the body from past experiences and remembrance of them on the cellular level. This memory results in clenched fists and strained expression. Running in place makes you feel like you are doing something, but in reality one generates a lot of sweat and increases the heart rate, but one never moves, never progresses. Nothing appears to be changing outside the body, not the scene, not the circumstance. Feet are connecting with the past, being bodily mindful of it. The hands reaching forward with clenched fists expect more of the same in the future.

This textual reading makes it very well positioned for linking it to consumption of consumer goods. Consumer spending, individuals and households, comprises the majority of profit for corporations, and provides more than half of the gross domestic and national products for this country. Advertisements and marketing campaigns are used to target specific consumers in specific categories. Consumption spending typically comes from people who work. In this context I define those who work as those who would be homeless after missing three paychecks, or those who do not have significant liquid savings to hold them over in downturned economic times, for at least one year. Homelessness in this definition includes living with someone when one's name is not on the lease, mortgage or other legal document showing financial responsibility for the given dwelling. As such this categorization of worker includes people who are considered middle class. Consumers are bombarded with media advertisements encouraging them to buy, with messages that indicate they are deficient if they do not. Deficiencies can easily be overcome by consuming with credit cards, being charged usury levels of interest.

This consumer culture has been exported around the globe resulting in an imagined community of laborers often in debt, those who have been lulled into the belief that hard work will enable better consumption, and escape from the toil of being a laborer. It is such a myth of Sisyphus metaphor, except Sisyphus knows his lot and accepts it. Those doing The Runnin Man neither know nor accept their lot. They run in ignorance. Many of these laborers work for subsistence in sweatshop conditions, when producing Nike tennis shoes or providing textile products out of China, or for examples, providing white collar outsourcing of legal services, call centers, and software development in India (George and Jones 2005). Of course we have seen examples of success stories, and this possibility cannot be ruled out.

Transformed into an *emic* text, laborers around the world do The Runnin Man because running in place is necessary in an increasingly global consumer culture. The metaphor is a strong one for capitalist consumption, theorized and documented by African Americans familiar with the process. In so doing writers were able to transmit this information to others both within their community and without. Moreover, the metaphor is perfect for driving consumption advertising messages.

The theory here is that African Americans write about their experiences in bodily form. Hip hop dance texts provide ways to learn more about the social history, the theories, and metaphors, the experiences of a group of people, strategies and tactics for dealing with life. At the same the text's language and message is quoted and used to seduce laborers into achieving capitalist ends. Understood textually, hip hop dance theorizes about consumerism, capitalist seduction, and the global exploitation of labor. In so doing, others are given mechanisms they can use to comprehend and adapt to events, and methods to deal with them. This is no different from using written texts to teach, make points, formulate theories, and persuade. When evaluated from this vantage point, hip hop dance texts are meaningful, rich, and worthy of documentation.

Viscous as this section has been, it has attempted to achieve certain ends. First it gave a history of hip hop dance and built upon it to theorize three texts. It has shown how there are double meanings found in the texts, and how the texts change when moved from African American writings and interpretations to another. In the case of The Runnin Man, the text went from *emic* to *etic* to *emic* again, in support of the transportation of meaning theory suggested by Desmond, as discussed in the previous section. Rhetorical questions were raised when the texts were transmuted into pure *etic*, asking how they related to the historical and social contexts embedded in the text as written on African American dancers. Three texts were documented and some of their meanings and messages were theorized.

Tying It Together

The chapter opened with a discussion of a body that writes and gave a method for understanding what is being written. Especially we have to pay attention to choreographic intent and the creative processes involved in documents used for study. Texts need both skill and theory to be understood well, and moreover, when texts are given within a social context, they can be seen within an *emic* framework, going to the core of the issue of identity, forming a primary social text. Here the readers recognize differences and nuances within the language. When translated by other groups, understanding of this difference is watered down, if not altogether lost, unless the readers are capable of taking on the same or similar social histories and economic realities.

Like different kinds of texts provided in print, hip hop dance is spoken in Ebonics. This is so because of the existential present moment that the texts theorize. This is not to say that the texts are ephemeral, but rather to say that that they are not authorless, and require participation by members of the society. The language is constantly evolving, constantly developing new Significations and Signifyin. Nothing gets understood however, unless someone is there to read it and so we have the imagined community. That community has been expanding rapidly around the world and includes many different kinds of laborers who work within the capitalist world economy and basically have no choice in the matter. Hip hop dance taken out of context has been matched with product placements and consumption. *Emic* texts such as The Runnin Man, The Snake and The Cabbage Patch, as theorized in this chapter, really have nothing to do with consumption. *Etic* texts have everything to do with it.

Notes

1. There has been much discussion on the topic of essentializing and anti-essentializing and the problems associated with these extremes (see Gilroy 1993, for example). I do not want to enter into this debate, only drive home my position with regard to hip hop dance.

2. Existentialism in Ebonics would be considered "Funk" as suggested by Cornel West and discussed in De Frantz (2004). As my own metaphysical interpretation of this, Funk connects movement with text and places the loci in the here and now, keeping authors and writers in communication with at least one other person.

3. See the note in the Preface to this book, and also refer to Roland Barthes and Stephen Heath, trans., *Image Music Text*, Hill and Wang, 1977; Michel Foucault "What is an author?" *Partisan Review*, 4, 603–613, 1975, for a full discussion of the ideology of the death of an author.

4. This structure of rap, dance, and graffiti reflects what Thomas DeFrantz points out in his essay *The Black Beat Made Visible* (2004). He suggests, following Pearl Primus' work, that within the African and African American tradition, we have a tricotomy: orality, dancer, drum. These same structures are present in hip hop.

5. The reader is invited to look into the essay by Katrina Hazzard-Gordon *Dancing Under the Lash: Sociocultural Disruption, Continuity and Synthesis* (1998) for a discussion of the power slaves achieved for themselves in dancing. At issue in this citation for purposes of the work at hand is to show that availing power has been used this way in black America for centuries, and that it is intertextually connected to what we are seeing in hip hop dance.

6. Please read Anderson's text if you have an interest. He covers historical communities, racism, mapping and a number of issues that help one understand the reach of capitalism and the aspects the system uses to achieve its ends. It is really fascinating but the depth of it is beyond my scope here.

7. Here I am reminded of *Sweetness and Power* by Sidney Mintz (1985). In that work Mintz showed the ways in which sugar became associated with the success of the working classes, and how the working classes had many problems associated with buying into relating consumption of sugar and sugar products. Some of those problems included poor health, but more importantly the problem of large scale disillusionment due to the fact that consumption of sugar did not make a poor person wealthy. The production of it did.

8. See Eric N. Berkowitz, *et al.*, *Marketing*, 7th edition, Irwin/McGraw Hill: Boston, 2003, for a full discussion on marketing, corporations, and globalization.

9. Timothy Havens has produced an outstanding article (2002) on the ways in which television programming using blacks is distributed. There he covers decisions that are made in the US by individuals who perceive the value of black situation comedies, how budgets for production of programs are small relative to comparable white programming, and how cultural difference influences what is aired internationally. Specifically Havens addresses the ways in which race and language are commodified globally for profit. His research covered markets in a wide variety of first, second, and third world countries.

2

African Diaspora

The parts ... on which their shackles are fastened, are often
excoriated by the violent exercise they are thus forced to take...,
even those who had the flux, scurvy, and such oedematous
swelling in their legs as made it painful to them to move at all,
were compelled to dance by the cat.

— Alexander Falconbridge,
quoted by Lynne Emery,
*Black Dance in the United States
from 1619 to 1970* (Emery 1972, 8)

This pain might best be described as the history that hurts —
the still-unfolding narrative of captivity, dispossession, and
domination that engenders the black subject in the Americas.

–Saidiya Hartman,
Scenes of Subjection (1997, 51)

What we are privileged to witness here is the (political, seman-
tic) confrontation between two parallel discursive universes.

— Henry Louis Gates, Jr.,
The Signifying Monkey (1988, 45)

*Imagine yourself on a ship during the period between the mid–1400s
to the late 1800s. You have no clothes and there are so many other people
on the ship that you can barely turn around in place. If you are a woman,
you may be menstruating, in labor, or at any stage of reproductive cycling.
Or, you may have just recently been raped. You may be seasick. If not seasick, then you may be sick from the stench of thousands of people held in*

a space who have not been allowed to bathe for weeks, from the stench of excretions ranging from defecation to vomit. You are hungry, thirsty, tired and terrified. Spoken language is incomprehensible to you. No paper or pen to write with and even if there was, there is no one to send your writing to. And then you get mad, madder, angry. Recognize your powerlessness. No land in sight. If you try to jump off the ship, you may or may not know how to swim but even if you do you will be re-captured and beaten for trying to escape. Though it might be your full wish, unfortunately you may not be killed in the process.

The people who are with you, who you are chained and shackled with, you have never seen before. You do not know where you are going but you know you have been captured. The ship is filthy and the white men running the ship are filthier both inside and outside. Their demeanor holds nothing good and they will rape anybody. Their primary purpose is to get your body to a point of sale. Having you arrive alive and salable for a sufficient profit is uppermost in their minds. In order to make this sale profitable, you have to be in a certain physical condition. Therefore, the white men make you "dance."

In their desire to achieve their overriding goal, the white men bring you up to the deck of the ship and using whips make you dance. You have to move like you like moving, pretend that you enjoy doing it or else you will be flogged with the whips. The chains on you ankles are not removed for this purpose and so your ankles are bleeding from the friction of the shackles locked around you and your companions. And it is not a dance that you have practiced in your homeland rituals for sacred summonses, secular celebrations or ancestral worship. It is a dance of despair, force, and humiliation which documents the environment you now face, references the place you left, and theorizes about where you are going.

Change

In this chapter hip hop dance is linked to a social history reading and an interpretation of the Diaspora from Africa. Language, the educational system, and the effects of the ways in which African Americans were and are socially limited are discussed pursuant to the dance.

The reason for this is that it would be beneficial if people continue, or begin as the case may be, to value individual and collective intelligences of African Americans. A different reading of African American bodies and contexts is begging for exposure. It needs to be understood that this African American collective body, and the individual people that comprise it, are assets in and of themselves, and own assets within their bodies and within their brains. Written on African American bodies and internalized in African American brains are struggles and trials differing for men and women, according to the various segments of African American society one belongs to.

A short list of the difficulties accruing to African American women can be thought of without much effort. Rape, domestic or other violence from family, friends, husbands, or strangers. Robbery with or without rape. Marginalization resulting in not getting the job; or get the job, be "the only one" there and thus be called a lesbian or be called a feminist or an Ann. Worse, somebody may get to talking loosely about the ho they saw on Friday night, forgetting themselves and it being too late to take the words back. Meanwhile, at home and in the hood they may think she is nothing but a bougie. On the financial front, she wonders will that e-loan go through and at the lowest interest rate since now that everyone has to show a photograph, thank you the Patriot Act? Will all the neighbors move out when I move in or will I move out when the blacks move in?

African American men have problems to think about too that have provided sources of theoretical management structures within their bodies, for example, "Driving While Black," being caricatured as a sexual deviant, and being categorized as unemployed and unemployable. As such then he must be a drug dealer with gold teeth. He nevertheless is seen as ignorant, but belligerent and dangerous. Placed in opposition to African American women. Looked upon as a pimp. At work he may face sexual harassment charges, violence in the workplace, or any number of corporate strategies that undermine self-esteem that ultimately results in termination for cause.

There are few, if any, places on Earth where African Americans can go and not be discriminated against, that is few places where one can arrive and not be reminded of the negative text images associated with and marked on those bodies. Sometimes the discrimination is so subtle it takes a while before it is recognizable. These discriminatory practices that happen around the globe result from enslavement, real and media driven. True, not only Africans and African Americans experience racism and discrimination; it happens to all manner of people, but as has already been said, the focus of this work is on African Americans.

How

Edward Thorpe in his 1989 book entitled *Black Dance* reminds us that the emancipation of slaves came into force sometime between 137 and 171 years ago. "Even so, Black people in the western world have remained enslaved by the forces of politics, prejudice and poverty" (Emery 1989, 9). Between their launch from the coast of Africa and their arrival in the Americas, it was common practice for slaves "to be taken first to the West Indies and the islands of the Caribbean" (Emery 1989, 9) where Africans picked up ways of writing dances and theorizing their existence. This trajectory from Africa to the West Indies and the Caribbean influenced the text of African American dances from early enslavement and continues to do so today.

Hazzard-Donald (1996) further described African dances in the New World as containing "biting commentary" (Hazzard-Donald 1996, 221). By analogy and through intertextuality, hip hop dance can be said to be making biting commentary. For example, in the previous chapter The Snake was theorized. Through intertextuality, the dance can be read as teaching both a rural and industrial history, giving biting commentary in its literature: one that records and gives direction about living with the lash of enslavement as well as time spent in maneuvering through urban racism. Hazzard-Donald tells us, "Like a language, the basic vocabulary of African American dance is passed along" (Hazzard-Donald 1996, 222). In this it could be inferred that the history that is not always accepted in spoken or written form in the main is spoken and sent on as a dance. It serves as a citation for future dance writings.

These messages that are transmitted have to appear in ways that are acceptable to the white power establishment. Thus, as Hazzard-Donald reported, African American dances were coded in ways that kept the performer-choreographers from drawing the wrath of powerful whites that "bore a stamp of theatrical and plantation subservience" (Hazzard-Donald 1996, 222) by the way African Americans physically wrote with their bodies stooped over. As African Americans acquired some measure of freedom, the bodily texts became more upright. In any period of African American dance, and particularly in hip hop dance, encoded messages contained signified commentary about Euro-Americans themselves. A few African American social dances that pre-date hip hop dance, but from which hip hop dance draws, include The Lindy Hop, The Jerk, and The Pop Lock. The Lindy Hop for example, teaches that yes, African Americans have suffered much racism and oppression, but that we no longer have to bend and bow down to that oppression. We can lift each other up and over it. The Jerk metamor-phasized into The Pop Lock. The discontinuity, lack of stability, and certain insecurity African Americans have faced throughout history, economically, politically and racially, is documented here.

Other moves that are characteristic of hip hop dance are those such as freezes and stances. They can be read as action verbs when read correctly. For example, as in the case of the freeze, it says take note of what your surroundings are. This is something that African Americans have had to do, especially when running for freedom. On the other hand, the stance, one where the arms are crossed over the chest and the body is slightly leaning backwards with the weight placed mainly on one foot, means to wait, be confident in yourself, and get ready for the next move, as Hazzard-Donald would agree (Hazzard-Donald 1996, 231). As such, it could be interpreted as a sign that for the African American, that waiting has come to an end. It is time to take on and change oppression and economic disenfranchisement, and to brace against them.

Hazzard-Donald theorized break dancing — a misnomer of mass proportions coined by the media; the correct terminology is b-boyin or b-girlin and this classification will be the reference throughout the remainder of this book — as equal to the African American practice of playing the dozens, and displaying the physical manifestation of this through competitive movement practice with a distinct vocabulary. Additionally, that this form of hip hop dance reveals African American intelligence and quick wittedness, something that has been historically denied African Americans. If you have never played the dozens, or done a spin in b-boyin or b-girlin, an invitation is extended to you to try them so that you can experience the speed at which your mind must move to formulate intelligent remarks without rehearsal, or how physically fit you have to be in order to execute these physical dialogs. But the fact of the matter is that b-girlin and b-boyin was whitenized, introduced into mass media, renamed and picked off as an artifact called break dancing, capable of commoditization in the marketplace. The whitenizing consisted of removing the competitive, witty and intellectual aspects of the text and without which "breaking loses its thrust, its *raison d'etre*" (Hazzard-Donald 1996, 229). However, even with the watered down *etic* version written on Euro-American bodies, it nevertheless reveals and affirms the intellectual acumen characteristic of African Americans, and traces of the *emic* text remains visible to the skilled reader.

African American dance then has been packed with meaning and history since it began. And socio-economic forces have given rise to the types of dances being done. Hip hop dance arose out of this history and borrowed texts from the past and from different parts of the globe, coupled with the then-current economic realities of the late 1970s and early 1980s. What was occurring at the time was not only continued economic problems, but also a simultaneous decline in the African American family, a diminishing of African American male dominance in leading households, the first effects of desegregation, and a modernist (or post-modernist, depending on where you chose to be in time) move towards conspicuous consumption. Hip hop dance had to affirm both the individual and the group and demonstrate the value both have played in our survival over time. Thus you have the re-enactment of the cipher with the individual being supported within it. Realizing this need to embrace both the individual and the group in an economy increasingly reneging on gains made by African Americans, hip hop dance filled those voids.

Some writers on the topic of break dancing like to point out that there was little partnering going on during its genesis, and there was a setting aside of couple dances, as African American men were looking for answers to the social problems they faced. However what we witnessed in much hip hop dance was what Hazzard-Donald has termed "apart dancing." Apart dancing included b-boyin and b-girlin as well as later manifestations such as The Snake. In these types of dances, "the partners do not touch each other during the dance, yet the commitment to the partnering ritual is clear; this quality helps characterize both the traditional West African dance styles and many dance styles in African communities in the Americas." This "apart partner" dancing reveals a written text on how to be together but appear to be apart. Togetherness is important, but what is even more important is to not show too much interest in it, because of the certainty that getting comfortable as a couple or family provided a basis for being torn apart. Theorizing about being torn apart comes intertextually from enslavement, unemployment, racism, and other oppressive realities.

Many African Americans not only wrote about how to withstand being torn apart, but also wrote about challenging the oppressive social institutions. Hip hop dance has done much to present texts on defiance and change. Hazzard-Donald said,

> The richness of gesture and motion in hip hop dance ... reflects the effects of social and economic marginalization on their lives ... and [hip hop dance] simultaneously protects the participants from and represents a challenge to the racist society that marginalized them ... [H]ip hop dance poses an air of defiance of authority and mainstream society [1996, 229].

that has only ever been seen once during the Black Power movement of the sixties. At least in reporting history and current events, this method of pedagogy has not been completely shut down. Greg Dimitriadis also offers a path on which we may walk towards understanding hip hop dance texts as being a socio-economic-racial documentation *and* commentary on events changing over time. In his "Hip Hop: From

Live Performance to Mediated Narrative" which appeared in the second volume of *Popular Music* in 1996, he wrote

> The role of dance in hip hop history ... is often understated or ignored, especially by critics with logocentric biases.... The body itself is often ignored or dismissed.... [N]ew ways of being in the world ... can thus be located and nurtured in and through the body.... The body can connect with "experiential worlds" different from those articulated by dominant orders.... Individuals exploring different ways of being in collective contexts is the prelude and precursor to all important social or political action. Hip hop club activity in the late 1970s thus offered sites of resistance as potent as ... protest discourses.... Hip hop engages the postmodern present in its stress on the discontinuous and the contingent while it nurtures a community building musical tradition rooted in the oral.... Hip hop [is] a concrete experience all about the particulars of a complex multi-tiered social event [1996, 180–184].

Turning now to another scholar's work to examine movement, phrasing, statements, and how they integrate to make meaning, consider A.L. Austin. Austin's field of study was philosophy and he gave several lectures in 1955 which were subsequently published in 1962 as *How to Do Things with Words*. Austin probed sentence structures and statements, and one of his central ideas is that some utterances "record or impart straightforward information about the facts" (Austin 1962, 2) and some state observations about the circumstances in which they are said. Not only that, but statements are subject to constraints and the context in which they are said. This is not rocket science so far. However proceeding beyond this, he posits that performative sentences are those sentences in which the body supports what the mouth is saying, and, "In very many cases it is possible to perform an act of exactly the same kind by not uttering words ... but in some other way.... To say something is to do something" (Austin 1962, 8, 12). While Austin stops short of making the connection between how the "other ways of saying something," i.e. with the body and not with the mouth or pen, relate to "to say something is to do something," manipulation of his philosophizing about utterances onto African American dancing bodies is imperative. An example will make it clear.

We have gestures of the body that are culturally specific. When we motion with our hand and arm to wave "Hello," or when two of us meet for the first time or after a long absence, we shake hands or embrace. These utterances of the body without using words are doing something and saying something. It would be difficult to utter "Hello" with a wave if we kept our hands in our pockets, perhaps. Without the movement there is no statement of "Hello." The same argument could be made for giving someone a hug. And notice that an everyday common body statement, such as an embrace or a wave "Hello" are readable only in a community setting and require a set of particular circumstances. I would be thought insane if I stood there shaking an imaginary hand, or if in my home I waved "Hello" to introduce myself to myself. Or, it would be odd to introduce myself or extend a greeting by a handshake to a family member that I live with.

Similarly, hip hop dances contain statements, interrogatives, phrases and punctuation, strung together uttered with the body that "say something by doing something." Dances are uttered in a socio-cultural set of circumstances — African village, slave ship, plantation, inner city, you name it — and function properly only if being read by another literate reader of these types of utterances. To listeners not familiar with the phrases and meanings, hip hop dance utterances appear as movements without intent that develop out of nowhere and disappear when the movements and the music stops.

Socio-cultural familiarity is not the only circumstance involved in hip hop dance saying something. Oppression and lack of economic advancement are characteristics that are necessarily integral factors within the system of capitalism. The related strategy stacks up such that some people have wealth, and others do not. The carrot tied to that strategic stick is that if one works hard (thereby supporting capitalism) one could also one day be wealthy.

Joining oppression and economic lack in capitalists' strategies are domination and control. Inseparable from the strategy of capitalism, they are designed to make people under the system believe in structures of power. Members at the bottom — those with no power, no money and no control — find ways to tactically poke holes in the system. Holes poked in the system become what the tacticians produce outside strategic production (de Certeau 1984). During the slave economy enslaved workers who produced agricultural products rebelled tactically by eating sugar, something that was forbidden by the strategists (Mintz 1986). Similarly, strategically unemployed, racially ill-favored and historically oppressed African Americans in the inner city tactically undermined the academic system by producing commentary — written bodily — in spaces not intended for such writing.

The tactic of dancing on street corners because there was no other place, along with the tactic of scratching to make new music by artists so that they would not incur hard costs, exploded into a worldwide demand for a body saying something. Capitalism naturally found a way to exploit the products created outside the system. But uncommercialized hip hop dance (and rap) remains tactical through the messages and history inscribed on and inscribed by a dancing body's products.

Another way of understanding power relationships and hip hop dance comes through anthropologist David Kertzer. In his 1988 *Ritual, Politics and Power*, Kertzer undrapes roles that rituals play in politics and the concomitant maintenance of power. He informs the reader that rituals are not merely subjects of supernatural or spiritual practices witnessed on certain vacations or on ethnographic excursions. In secular life they not only maintain power but give meaning to existence for a given community of people. For example, the recent run on the market for buying up American flags gave meaning to some in the aftermath of the September 11, 2001, terrorist attacks in the New York and Washington, D.C. areas. Literally, you could not buy a flag during a certain period of time after the attacks if your life depended on it. Albeit that flags are symbols, the ritual of sporting the American flag on buildings, cars, shoes, clothes, electric and non-electric billboards, on buses, etc., reinforced (some) Americans' belief in US leaders. They symbolized the purchasers' faith in the US power structure to both defend them from social deviants and to see the US as all-powerful, as well as to reinforce American citizen solidarity. The symbolic meaning of the American flag obviously is conveyed in a nonverbal form, and gains credence through a play on history, power, and in this case, emotions.

Just as particular political rituals and symbols stand as non-verbal signals reinforcing power, Kertzer notes, "rituals are also important for revolutionary groups who must ellicit powerful emotions to mobilize the people for revolt" (Kertzer 1988, 14). Stirred emotions show up as statements and acts by oppressed groups demonstrating their lack of acceptance of the regiment of power, that the power structure is not natural and can be changed. But by the same token, Kertzer is quick to point out the fact that rites, rituals and certain acts of rebellion also reinforce the dominant power structures.

A case in point is that under certain circumstances aboard slave ships, there were uprisings and attempted revolts by the enslaved. During their time on the deck when being forced into the required ritual of dancing to ensure profitability, many of the enslaved attempted escape. Most who attempted this failed; if caught they were beaten unmercifully or killed. Or if not captured, many drowned. Thus rebellion or revolution against enslavement and the required ritual of enslaved dance reinforced the power structure of capitalism, making bodies commodities.

While hip hop dance initially had its texts labeled as rebellious, able to evoke a revolution in regards to socio-economic and racial oppression, it quickly became usurped into reinforcing capitalism, happening quickly with respect to rap music and somewhat more slowly for danced texts. Nevertheless, hip hop dance texts combined the force of emotional and mental understandings of centuries of oppression and articulated bodily phrasing meant to spin capitalism around on its head and shoulders, and popped the locks of power (at least momentarily) so that African Americans knew that they did not have to go along or all get along under the guise of Western power structures.

African Americans then, in writing hip hop dances, made philosophical statements, interpreted economic theory, and tactically twisted ritual power to their advantage. The trouble lies in reading the codes of the movement vocabulary. What came to pass with the revolution communicated through Africanist bodies was what always comes to pass with African American genius: it got sold until it was unrecognizable as belonging to African Americans.

Strategic, Tactical, Commercial

Explicitly clear is that there is a difference between hip hop dance written for tactical and strategic purposes and hip hop dance staged for commercial ones. Commercial hip hop dance is used in movies, videos, sit-coms, and concerts, to facilitate sales, sex, and identity. Sometimes you find endeavors that primarily address hip hop dance; for example Rennie Harris' *PureMovement* stages hip hop dance through a proscenium. Appreciably Harris provides a remembrance space for tactical hip hop dance: bodies re-enacting what used to take place and perhaps still does at block parties and on street corners of inner cities. Harris also stages choreographed work that gives audiences a view of hip hop dance virtuosity unrivalled by the best athletes, including Kobe and Shaq. What you have in a live proscenium though is a restaging, sort of a reconstructed reading of a text. "Live" freestyle hip hop dance "audiences" write, whereas proscenium audiences passively absorb the texts. There is no "audience" per se in "live" hip hop dance where dialog occurs and history is written.

Additionally, you have to be mindful of what you are reading when watching electronic portrayals such as videos, movies, sit-coms or other choreographed second-degree hip hop dance. You must be able to recognize a statement that includes a fleeting Runnin Man or Roger Rabbit, or a Sea Walk hidden in a "grapevine" versus a Crip Walk. And you have to be able to identify and read punctuation, like a freeze or a lean or a chin rub. While all hip hop dance staged in a proscenium may not be new social commentary, but both an *emic* or *etic* depending on the audience's reference point, remember that hip hop dance on the street corner or in other social settings, like clubs, i.e., *emic*, is. Just as the dances of the enslaved were. For example, those enslaved who were forced to dance on the slave ship wrote texts of resistance when dancing because total resistance to the requirement to make movement on demand was read by slavers as too much resistance. Instead of outright resistance then, the enslaved wrote their paragraphs which documented the requirement to move on command while at the same time making a social commentary about the absurdity of the requirement. Enslaved people were not told that they had to move a certain way, only that they had to move. They danced in a ring, in their chains "writhing and twisting in 'disgusting and indecent attitudes'" (Emery 1972, 11). Slavers wrote these types of phrases in their notebooks, and other entries like it, while the enslaved wrote with their bodies and were written upon. And so like the dictator, before the first coming of Christ, over the Syracusians who believed that the best subjects were silent subjects, and whose constituents began to talk and signify with their bodies, enslaved people talked and signified with their bodies and at the same time defied the language barrier that existed between themselves and their captors.

A present day example of a text writing with resistance is The Dog. It may have a connection to Snake Hips. In mainstream media this dance has been read as a sexual dance. The dance as commoditized is about black women's sexuality and the motion of sexual intercourse standing on one's feet. It is the most co-opted dance that one can see on music videos and even in middle-class white high school auditoriums made open for talent shows and dance performances. Many African Americans who actually perform The Dog, though, provide a much needed message of reinforcing positive self-esteem. More about The Dog will come later.

So unstaged and staged hip hop dance is like the difference between having an excellent conversation or argument or shout — complete with Signifyin — and having to make a speech or participate in a pre-planned debate. Part of the importance of a satisfying African American conversation is for the participants to exchange, document, understand, support, not support, disagree, agree, curse, and so on over racism, sexism, religion, politics, relationships, discrimination, lack of education, drugs, AIDS, affirmative action, OJ, etc. In a speech, you are practiced, statements are memorized, points are covered from notes made for the occasion. You are nervous. Or, it is similar to how rappers talk about freestyling: just get up to the mike, rap, be clever and make a statement. Many of them say that planned rap, though it does make a statement, is not as packed with meaning as freestyle rap lyrics. A choreographed hip hop dance has the same elements of structure and planning, but the statement the dance makes comes off as weak.

White people have enjoyed watching Africans and African Americans dance for centuries. It is no surprise that they now like watching us dance in multimedia representations. And it is common knowledge that white people like watching other white people imitate black people. They dressed themselves up in blackface and pretended to be black (a black for a day experience) and white people flocked to see these performances.[1] It is no different with hip hop dance. Caucasians still love to see African American dance, and spend millions of dollars making sure they can. Because when witnessing a dance text that is African American in design it stands out unless it has been watered down to the point where you have to dig for it, like Brenda Dixon Gottschild did.

Language Used in Thinking and Writing

If hip hop dance is a tactic against the strategy of domination and power, what should we say about Ebonics? There is a whole system of language growing tactically — worldwide thanks to the media and capitalism — alongside the dominant one even with the effort of the dominant to squelch, appropriate and imitate African Americans without giving proper credit or even understanding what they have or what they are saying.

Rappers speak in Ebonics and as such have made certain words and phrases part of the English language, much like "Bojangles" Robinson did with "copasetic."

Consider this. Standing in a hip hop dance club in Rotterdam, The Netherlands, I notice the Euro-American Bouncer doing The Runnin Man while the African-descended DJ scratches rap by artists Ja-Rule and Snoop Dog on the wheels of steel. "Yo, Dogg, whas-up?" says the Bouncer to the DJ. They speak Dutch in The Netherlands! In a small town called Chicoutimi, Quebec, I took a hip hop dance class (which they labeled "Funky Dance — Advanced") from a pale-skinned French-speaking Canadian and I was the only African-descendent student. He had the Ebonics down while he was teaching class. "Gimme some tude, yall!" he yelled in between counting "un, deux, trois, quatre, cinq, six, sept, huit." In Cancun, Mexico, I "wave yo hands in the air, wave em like you jus don't care — say hoooooOOOO" following the orders of the DJ at a hip hop dance club. These now worldwide tactics called hip hop dance and Ebonics teach not only African American history but teach whole groups of dominated people how to resist tactically. But more importantly, people speaking Ebonics and writing hip hop dance texts teach African American history in present day contexts.

As you know, from the slave ship, the enslaved were sold to various peoples throughout the world. This is not to negate or ignore the notion that many African people were free people and not brought to the New World in this manner. But most African people, about nine million or so, were dispersed globally in this way in support of capitalism. Many scholars and writers have shown how dances of African Diasporaed people kept reference to dances done in their homelands. For example, Emery (1972), Malone (1996), and Hazzard-Gordon and Hazzard-Donald (1990, 1996) have all demonstrated the connections of historical movement texts to present day social dances done from the Middle Passage to plantation dances, from black balls and minstrelsy, to social dances done in urban areas.

Enslaved people performed dances for masters, for God, and for each other. Circle dances, the Cake Walk, cotillion dances, minstrelsy, tap dance, Snake Hips, call and response dances, dirty dancing, the Charleston, Zydeco, Lindy Hop, the Mashed Potato, The Jerk, The Hitchhike, The Rock Steady, The Bump, The Funky Chicken, The Point, The Wiggle and so on can all be shown to possess certain elements of syncopation, layering and rupture directly related to the intertextual manner of writing done by Africans before they were required to "dance" on slave ships.

Can our hip hop dances — The Crip Walk, The Sea Walk, The Snake, The Electric Slide, The Bounce, The Roger Rabbit, The Runnin Man, The Cabbage Patch, The Dog, The Box Step, The Pop Lock, The Robot, and The Harlem Shake — be thoughts and social commentary connected to the African Diaspora written in Ebonics?

The enslaved probably did not speak whatever language the enslavers spoke and in many cases because they were taken from diverse locales in Africa, they probably could not speak to each other in words. The black dance history book writers, quoting from writings of slave traders, tell us that they sang "melancholy lamentations of their exile from their native country" (Emery 1972, 8). But since these songs were not in the slaver's language, how did he know what they were singing about? It must have been a feeling.

Did you know that the National Association of Speech Pathologists recognizes Ebonics as a language?[2] Many African Americans speak Ebonics among friends and relatives. If you have ever traveled to a foreign country where people do not speak your native language, you know how good it feels to be amongst people who can keep up with your speed of talking and blending of words, contractions of sentences, innuendos, humor, and so on. The same is true for speakers of Ebonics. But there is a tremendous controversy surrounding it.

Just like there are many African Americans who do not dance or have rhythm, there are many African Americans who cannot speak Ebonics. (It is from the notion that all the enslaved were forced to dance that gives rise, I think, to the notion that all African-Diasporaed people can dance. There are many millions of African-Diasporaed people who could not execute an African American social dance even if their mama said they could not eat dinner until they did. So I want to avoid the essentializing idea that all African American people can and do dance.) Not surprisingly to me at least, there are many African Americans who are against the idea of speaking it. (We should not be shocked by this since there are also African Americans who think the displacement of Affirmative Action was a good idea, but really we ought not be disquieted by these things because all African Americans are not alike.) For so many years the black person who could not enunciate or articulate the King's English was ridiculed. Many of our parents and great-grandparents wanted to beat the slurs, axes, caints, and dems out of us. That viewpoint is valid and deserves consideration and respect. But those same slurs, axes, caints and dems form a rich language. Those language nuances are the same types of nuances that make hip hop dance say something.

I was watching a video about hip hop dance and culture and when the African Americans or African-Jamaicans were speaking, nice little English subtitles appeared at the bottom of the screen when the interviewees responded to questions in Ebonics. Because it is my native language, communicating in Ebonics comes much easier for me than in standard English. Similarly it has been shown that taking tests in Ebonics for many African American children demonstrates their intelligence rather than their ignorance. My ease of communicating in Ebonics compared to English, my ease of writing hip hop dance texts, and African American children's increased self-esteem from scoring highly on standardized tests written in Ebonics simply points to the fact that all languages have structures that facilitate communication. Many African American children taking standardized tests written in English are, for all intents and purposes, taking their tests in a foreign language.

A body moving is a body writing and writing is a bodily occurrence; hip hop dance is not written in English, but rather it is written in Ebonics. And this is why some people read The Dog as they do, or why certain stances are read as belligerent or even why some African American people do not want their children listening to rap or doing hip hop dance. Hip hop dance is an Ebonics teaching through black, brown and cream colored bodies, a historical account of the events of history left out of written in English American history texts.

There has been extreme controversy over the mere idea that African Americans can have their own language, and the theoretical words here offered surely will not minimize it. Ebonics comes from enslaved people who spoke a different language trying to learn English and therefore it has elements of both languages. But certainly Ebonics has a structure just as French or Spanish or German have structures. Unfortunately for some African American children in the United States though, we are not given language lessons like those we would receive if we were going to learn a Romance, Germanic or Slavic language. When language acquisition is sought, one first learns words in the native language that mean the same things in the language being acquired. Verb tenses, placement of nouns and pronouns and general sentence structure comes next. And if you have ever attempted to become fluent in a language other than your native tongue, you know full well how difficult it is. But for many African American children, instead of being taught English systematically, the education process is given in English. Children are told they are stupid, told that they must articulate more, enunciate more, study harder and longer. Failure often occurs and instead of there being a change in the educational process, many African Americans, feeling inadequate, turn away from education altogether.

Inadequacy follows many of us that do chose to go to college. We are first told that we have to pass a standardized test that is in a foreign language. Many of the written sections of these examinations are difficult for the most fluent English speaker to synthesize. If we squeak by with a decent score we embark upon a college career where the matriculation rate for African Americans is ridiculously low. We are given texts to read in colleges and universities that are in English, told that writing and understanding math and science requires a command of Standard English grammar and any attempt to write or theorize or hypothesize in Ebonics results in failure.

This can be seen in the controversy generated by an Oakland, California, School District's resolution in 1996 which established Ebonics as a language that needed to be recognized in addressing the educational needs of its African American children. Teachers not fluent would have been required to learn Ebonics and teach African American children as if they were learning French or Spanish or German or Japanese, etc. Federal legislators, as a result of the Oakland School District's proactive attempt to provide not only greater opportunity for the 25,000 African American children in their district to attend college, but also to reduce the suspension rate, the number of African American children labeled special needs or suffering from Attention Deficit Disorder, were quick to adopt policy blocking any education dollars that would support the acceptance and teaching of Ebonics in any school in the United States. Before the Oakland School District debacle a similar progression of events occurred in Ann Arbor, Michigan, in 1978.

I. Hip Hop Innovation

June Jordan gave a 1985 account of the negativity her students faced in attempting to publish an article in the newspapers, in Ebonics, that spoke to police brutality of African American youth. You already know that no newspaper would publish the students' Ebonics language editorial about an African American student who was killed through police brutality. Hip hop rappers have taken the tack that rap music is the newspaper, the CNN of their communities, and Ebonics is the language it is published in. Hip hop dance functions as a medium of communication for social circumstances and events in a physical Ebonics, published on street corners, clubs, homes, and, more palatable for those who have issues with blacks, published in music videos, sit-coms, movies and hip hop dance instruction videos.

Certain parents of African Americans, especially those of certain generations, often made the case to their children to distance themselves from bad English so that they would not be considered stupid. Many people also connect Ebonics with paragraphs of dirty language, and here I am reminded of an Orbit Gum commercial recently aired wherein Snoop Dogg (dressed in regular hip hop attire, speaking to an auditorium full of teen-aged upper class boys, mainly white but a few are ethnic, dressed in preparatory school uniforms, boys who are looking at Snoop Dogg with their jaws dropped as he tells them what it is like to be a gangster player pimp), finds himself suddenly transported to hell, with three white women all dressed in devil's outfits, red, complete with horns on their heads. These deviled white women size him up, pass judgment, and then give Snopp Dogg a piece of Orbit Gum to clean up his language. The tagline is stated by a white girl dressed in white: "Dirty Mouth? Clean it up with Orbit Gum." Snoop Dogg immediately ascends to what would be characterized as heaven, where all the white women are wearing white, chewing white gum, Snoop Dogg has on white, and is speaking rightly white — not saying a word that is.

But the fact of the matter is that even with an excellent command of English many African Americans who are accomplished often face people who consider them stupid anyway before they even open their mouths. Hip hop rappers threw themselves into writing songs that exclusively utilized Ebonics. Phrases now show up in other languages other than English and speakers of these crossover words pretend that those words did not come from Ebonics. We all know that "*ménage à trois*" is French, "*gesundheit*" is German, and "*quesadilla*" is Spanish. Words and phrases like "bad," "big time," "he got game," "bank," "chill," "don't go there," "go girl," "the hood," "twenty-four-seven," "It's a [girl/guy/whatever/whoever] thang," and "he got it going on" are some examples of Ebonics words, phrases and idioms that have crossed over into mainstream English. Even on my university campus all students are invited to sessions called "Rappin' with the Chancellor" where they can get their feelings out and express their concerns directly to the chancellor. You can see parking spaces in Kansas City that say "No Parking 24-7." And while watching Tiger Woods play in the 2002 Buick Open golf tournament I heard Buick's advertising tagline, "It's all good." Another advertisement for custom wheels, broadcasted on television, indicated that they would make your "ride" look right.

Meaning comes from language, which structures our reality, and the way we conceptualize the world is dependent on the language we speak. Rap singers speak in Ebonics, which comes to terms with racism and oppression and the fact that Africans could not speak English when they were cabbaged, and for centuries we were not allowed education. By the same token, hip hop dance is a performed Ebonics which stems from historical movement vocabularies. These concepts of history making can be made clear if we look at time values associated with the study of language. Hip hop dance in Ebonics diachronically writes on bodies.

Language is also divided into *parole* and *langue*. Langue is the system of language itself, while parole is the individual use or utterances of language (Barthes 1977). *Langue* and *parole* are the same as structure and performance. Hip hop dance grew out of b-boyin and b-girlin which was accompanied by rap songs. Rap speaks of the structure of oppression and racism and hip hop dance performs it. Whether one is well versed in the system of language (oppression and racism) and fluent in its utterances (movement history of oppression and racism) does not matter if the language and dance are treated as inferior. The system of language is ignored and the utterances ciphered.

I. Hip Hop Innovation

Hip hop dance and Ebonics are direct descendants of communication tools developed by enslaved Africans in America. Both language and movement vocabularies tend to be deemed less important than vocabularies written with the hand, spoken with the mouth. Texts written in unrecognized languages such as Ebonics and misread movement practices called hip hop dance, as of today, cannot be seriously served up in a court of law as evidence, cannot be seriously used to take college entrance examinations, cannot be legitimately used to make known the injustices of racism and sexism, and therefore cannot be theoretical and cannot theorize. Well, I and many other writers, hip hop dancers and rappers, disagree. Theorizing and theories are nothing but ways we try to make sense out of events, occurrences and observations. And in the words of Barbara Christian's 1990 contribution to *The Nature and Context of Minority Discourse*, African Americans "have always theorized but in forms quite different from the Western form of abstract logic" (Christian 1990, 38).

Wouldn't it be edifying, African American people, if we could take classes taught in Ebonics? How about translating Michel Foucault, or Roland Barthes or Jacques Derrida or Gayatri Spivak (or any of the theorists and philosophers) into Ebonics? Or chemistry, math, computer science, anthropology, engineering and physics with examples that are relevant to African Americans? The purpose of doing this would be to give value to the language that many of us speak, build credence for a way of being that is equally as valid as what the English institutions condone, and perhaps thereby contribute to self-esteem of an entire race. How about using Ebonics and hip hop dance to teach dance theory and history? Using these to teach theory would provide a strong addition to critical theories and their explanations of signification and the choreographies of writing.

But this is impossible to implement and I do not have to explain to you why. You know it intuitively. As such, hip hop dance and rap music took to the streets to demonstrate and communicate African American power, teach African American history, and current events of Euro and African America using the tools most available: body and voice.

2. African Diaspora

The language problem we face does not stop with college if we get there. The language problem manifests later in life in low employment, limited income, and limited educational opportunities. It follows us through careers. Let me put some statistics here for you to see what I am saying. I am putting demographic information here for the most current period of time for which this type of data were available at the time of this writing. The statistics indicate that African Americans do not fare well when compared to whites. This is no surprise. One reason, which is not obvious in these data, is that there is no strong representation of African Americans in places where it makes a difference. We witnessed that in the US presidential election of George W. Bush where many votes of African Americans were not counted — on purpose. James Brown knew the solution — he was theorizing — in the 1970s when he rapped on one of his songs, "we need a brand new funky president." That still has not happened. Perhaps Barak Obama (2008 black presidential candidate) will make it happen. Most major corporations are still headed by Euro-American men. We do not control economics or politics. These are the same circumstances that many of us faced when we were imported here from Africa. As the late The Notorious B.I.G. (a hip hop rapper who was killed) rapped, nothing has changed (Bad Boy Records 1997). But I am going to put these statistics here anyway. Understand that in most cases I have purposely not placed the data next to the corresponding statistics for Euro Americans. It is my belief that we do not need to compare ourselves to another American group but rather seek to take account of where we are and use that information to propel us forward. We know already that when data comparisons between African and Euro Americans are made, we have made very little progress in closing the many gaps that we have to straddle. And what does it mean, really, if Euro Americans get divorced at one rate and African Americans get divorced at another? What does it mean when we are more unemployed than Euro Americans? The information I am about to discuss is shown in Tables 2-1, 2-2, and 2-3.

Table 2-1. African American Population*

Approximate Number of Africans Dispersed to the US, 1440s–1860s	9,000,000		
Total Number of Americans	270,000,000		
African Americans	34,658,190	13%	of Total Americans
African Americans in Households	32,939,206	12%	of Total Americans
African Americans in Institutions	1,131,038	3%	of Total African Americans
African Americans in Other Living Arrangements	587,946	2%	of Total African Americans
African American Men	16,465,185		
African American Men in Households	15,204,383		
African American Men in Institutions	928,876	6%	of Total African American Men
African American Men in Other Living Arrangements	331,926		
African American Women	18,193,005		
African American Women in Households	17,734,823		
African American Women in Institutions	202,162	1%	of Total African American Women
African American Women in other living arrangements	256,020		

*Notes

Source: US Census, 2000.

The total number of Africans dispersed to North America and the corresponding dates have been estimated by Klein (1999). It is interesting to note that this estimate of 9,000,000 dispersed persons is equal to about 26 percent of the total African American population in the US as of 2000. "Institutionalized," according to the US Census, includes African American people under supervised care or custody; i.e., prisons, juvenile halls and nursing homes.

"Other," according to the US Census, includes African Americans in college dormitories, military and group homes.

Of the 928,876 African American Men in Institutions, 772,288 are between ages 18 to 49; 44,651 are under 18; 111,937 are over 50.

Of the 202,162 African American Women in Institutions, 78,837 are between ages 18 to 49; 10,131 are under 18; 113,194 are over 50.

Table 2-2. Where African Americans Live*

	South	Northeast	Midwest	West
African American residences	54.60%	18.70%	18.40%	8.30%
Non-Hispanic White residences	32.60%	20.20%	27.40%	19.80%

Metropolitan Areas

	Central City	Near Central City	Non-Metro area
African Americans	55.10%	31.00%	13.90%
Non-Hispanic Whites	21.70%	55.80%	22.50%

*Notes:
Source: US Census 1999
   Percentages are based on the total population of African Americans and Non-Hispanic Whites respectively.
   Figures do not include Institutionalized populations.

Table 2-3. African American Household Composition*

Household Size and Type

	Number of Persons			
	Two	Three	Four	Five or More
Married	33.70%	21.60%	24.00%	20.10%
Female, no spouse	37.40%	31.60%	17.40%	13.60%
Male, no spouse	62.30%	22.20%	72.00%	82.00%

*Notes:
Source: US Census Bureau, 1999.
   Based on 8.4 million African American Families: 47% are married-couple families, 45% headed by women, 8% headed by men.
   Percentages may not add up to 100 due to rounding.

Table 2-4. African American Education*

	Men	Women
Less than High School	23.30%	22.80%
High School Graduate	37.80%	34.00%
Some College	24.70%	26.80%
Bachelor's Degree or more	14.20%	16.40%

*Notes:
Source: US Census Bureau, 1999.
   Percentages may not add up to 100 due to rounding. Percentages based on African Americans over 25 years old.

If we take as a rough estimate that 9 million Africans were dispersed to the US, our population is almost four times as large, as of 2000, with 34,658,190 African Americans reporting in on the census.[3] There are 270 million total Americans, and African Americans represent 13 percent of the total population. Non-Hispanic whites comprise the majority of the American population, numbering about 193 million. Minorities may outnumber the majority in certain states, but we have a long way to go before minorities outnumber the majority on the whole. Of the 34 million or so African Americans, 1,131,038 or three-percent of us live in "institutions," read: "prisons" of one sort or another. Six percent, or 928,876, of the 16,465,185 African American men are in prisons and one percent of African American women spend their days in jail. There are 1,727,820 more African American women than men. For those of us that live outside institutions, we mainly live in cities and still are largely concentrated in the south.

Forty-five percent of the 8.4 million African American families are represented by married couples; next are single mother households, at 47 percent. African American men with no wives run eight percent of homes. A little over a third of African American women graduate from high school; the percentage is a little higher for African American men at almost 38 percent. However, percentagewise more African American women than men have advanced degrees. But I am going to come back to some of these statistics in the chapter "A Feminist Re-View of Hip Hop Dance." The majority of adult African Americans, some 85 percent of men and 83 percent of women, do not have college educations culminating in a degree of higher education. We need to get busy, and as Iyanla Vanzant says, "We got to get up from here" (Vanzant 2002 speech at Agape Los Angeles). These statistics are sad commentaries about Euro and African Americans, and I believe the lack of Ebonics texts and tools in teaching African Americans manifests itself in these statistics.

Do It to Say It

Some African Americans think that hip hop dance is just the latest mode of exploitation used against us, like the exploitation of blackface, or minstrelsy. However I think it is one of many dance texts in African America that can be seen in many contexts, different from the exploitation and negative connotations placed onto us in the past. I asked a question a few pages ago: Can our hip hop dances — The Crip Walk, The Sea Walk, The Snake, The Electric Slide, The Bounce, The Roger Rabbit, The Runnin Man, The Cabbage Patch, The Dog, The Box Step, The Pop Lock, The Robot and The Harlem Shake — be a response to the African Diaspora? In previous chapters The Snake, The Runnin Man, The Cabbage Patch were theorized. The dance movements were contextualized as to how they relate to the historical circumstances many African Americans face or have faced in their experiences in the United States. Those experiences result directly from enslavement and the institution of slavery which itself is predicated upon racism and sexism embedded in capitalism in this country, and the capitalist world economy. These dances are further direct discourses of the demographic data shown above. I am going to leave the theory about The Dog to the chapter on feminism and hip hop dance. So let me conclude this chapter by addressing here then The Robot, The Sea Walk, The Crip Walk, The Electric Slide, and The Harlem Shake.

A robot is a machine that has no intelligence of its own. The only way it performs its functions is by being programmed. Robots are built to do routine manual work that used to be done by human beings. They are operated automatically or by remote control and perform in a seemingly human way. African Americans were brought here to function as robots to do routine manual work the human beings (Euro Americans) did not want to do. African Americans were psychologically controlled to automatically operate at a certain production capacity, or by the remote control of the whip, and seemingly performed the tasks the human beings (Euro Americans) would have performed if they did not have their colored robots. Psychological remote control still haunts many African Americans, either from economic and educational despair or substance abuse or sexual abuse or homelessness or something else. Whips of unemployment and sexism still operate as a manner of remote control for many. The types of lives many of us live should not even be called human. The hip hop dance The Robot writes of these whips and psychological

scars. African American people have known bodily about a theory of internalized surveillance and domination for years, centuries (Foucault 1997). It is what is termed mental slavery. On the other hand, the dance can be seen as a theorizing about how to move away from the robotic slot into which capitalism places us. They may want us to be robots but in the dance the writer controls all of the vocabulary and establishes the space in which to compose sentences. People reading the dance therefore learn how to write history and apply it in other everyday contexts.

The Sea Walk. I almost feel like the name of that hip hop dance is self-explanatory. In case it is not, The Sea Walk tells the history of the Middle Passage. The feet are close together in this text and sort of shuffle next to each other; they are barely raised off the floor. At the end of a phrase, a slight hop is done as the writer advances a few centimeters away from the starting point, but at the end of the next phrase the writer moves back to the original starting point. At no time does the writer move outside of a radius of about the width of the shoulders, though the radius of movement begins at each new landing point at the conclusion of the phrase. The dancer can be far removed from the starting point, or can be in the same place at the end of the writing. Like other hip hop dances, The Sea Walk packs many movements of the body into one musical measure, so not only are the feet moving, but the hands, arms, torso, head and face are all contributing to the theorizing. Having a similar name but a making a different statement, I am told that The Crip Walk came from writings of a gang in the southern California area who called themselves Crips. This writing is simply the tracing of the names of the members of the gang, as well as the name of the gang itself, with the feet. It differs from The Sea Walk in that it writes of a more localized history of the reality of black on black crime in the inner city. At this point in time, neither The Crip Walk nor The Sea Walk has found its way into commercial or mainstream media representations of hip hop dance.

What can I say about The Electric Slide? You need at least three people to do this dance done in unison, and I think of it as a poetic writing celebrating group solidarity, teamwork, and mutual support by African Americans for each other. It is a series of movements in unison, the dancers alternating in direction, turning 360 degrees by the time one phrase is completed, with a four-count break that gives them the signal to turn or bow or slide. It is not uncommon to see 20 or 30 people doing The Electric Slide together at a party, and this dance is done at places with mixed audiences like your company office party, non-ethnic weddings, after award ceremonies, and so on. Even though the text is structured, there is a great deal of improvisation that goes on with many of the dancers, again packing as much movement into a four-count measure as possible. This dance can be done and often is performed with formal attire, such as wedding clothes, upscale evening wear, black-tie, after five and business suits. Not long ago I saw the phrase "The Electric Slide" on the screen of The Weather Channel when the two white meteorologists were forecasting thunderstorms across the Midwest, remarking to each other that people would not be dancing.

In summary, this chapter has related hip hop dance texts to the African Diaspora and the spoken language of Ebonics. It has theorized ways in which danced texts are used strategically, tactically, and commercially in negotiating African American quotidian life. Importantly, it has connected the texts with communication, both within and without the African American community. Statistics were presented clearly pointing out economic realities suggesting that those realities are a direct result of lack of African American access to education in an understandable language. Hip hop dance documents the social history related to these barriers.

Notes

1. I will cover the black-for-a-day phenomenon in detail as the book progresses. The idea is that aspects of blackness are for sale and purchase while the real issues and negative consequences of racism go unabated.

2. This language was referred to as Black Vernacular English by sociolinguists in the 1970s and 1980s, and had evolved into being called African American Vernacular English (AAVE) by the late 1980s. A large majority of African Americans use this language (Escalas 1994), the language called Ebonics (Williams and Grantham 1999), and "Sociolinguistic research has shown that AAVE is a complex, highly consistent dialect that follows grammatical rules to the same extent as do more socially accepted forms of English" (Escalas 1994, 304).

3. Hirschman and Hill (1999) estimated that the number of Africans involved in the slave trade was closer to 10 million.

3

A Feminist Re-view of Hip Hop Dance

Not long ago I was talking to an African American male friend about male dominance. My intimate friend is a college-educated, 40-something, financially average, attractive African American man, a "good man" who I am fond of who comes to my house by invitation. If he is there for dinner, say, he will sit on the couch and wait for me to serve him. I prepare the meal and he sits there. Then I serve the meal and he comes to the table. He sits down, at the head of the table—where I encourage him to sit, no less—and eats the food. He has not brought anything with him to thank me for the invitation. No bottle of sparkling apple cider, no bread, no nothing. So he sits down and eats. After he eats he returns to his perch on the couch. Will not set foot in the kitchen, does not offer to clear the table. When I tell him, in a way that reeks of me minding my mouth, "You can come in the kitchen, you know," he goes into the role of the wicked witch who melts from being hit with water.

I tell him that I have read works by excellent African American feminist writers and that I have learned so much from what they have said about the relationship between African American women and men. He tells me he is not interested in reading any male-bashing literature because he does not want to damage his psyche. That reading African American feminist writers is akin to reading literature that promotes white power, Nazism, and the inferiority of the black race. I do not take the cue and continue to press, without demanding anything. I ask him if he understands the way patriarchy has undermined relationships between African American men and women by making African American men think they should naturally dominate African American women and at the same time how African American women should naturally only be concerned with eradicating racism. Further, that patriarchal capitalism teaches labor oppression and sexual exploitation in the name of increased profits; that the only reason money has value is because we all agree that it has value. He says that he does not like the stigma that is associated with the term "patriarchy" and that lesbians want us to all believe that what is wrong with the world is all men's fault. That African American feminists just want to replace patriarchy with matriarchy. I tell him that matriarchy amongst African American women is a myth and how bell hooks has deconstructed the notion of African American women matriarchs by pointing out privileges a matriarch would enjoy if she were the head of some kingdom and that has never happened for African American women. He rebuts with the idea that, well, there are so many other things going on in the world, that there are so many things that we can disagree on — politics, religion, the Middle East — that we may just have to agree to disagree on this topic of male dominance. I say certain areas of understanding are so fundamental that agreeing to disagree means that we will have nothing to say to each other.

As a point of deconstruction, consider this rhetorical question. Why would someone else sign up and volunteer to be financially responsible for another able-bodied adult? That ideology again is a part of exploitative capitalism designed to control certain groups of people that we do not even question. It is not natural for a man to provide financial comforts for a woman. Imagine that you have to pay the way for another adult being all the time. That is a ridiculous operating system because eventually the payer wants something from the payee. Capitalism provides no free lunches. Eventually, the payer expects the payee to exchange something that payer perceives has an equivalent value for the efforts to financially support the payee. Such arrangements almost invariably lead to some kind of domination and control.

One view, one reading of sex does not have to be shoved down everyone's throat. The Euro American construction of sex is that it is bad, based on the original sin of a man who would not defend the woman he had.

Suppose that Adam had said, yes I took the fruit and I wanted her to get it for me, and that is my woman and what do you have to say about it, God? He did not do this and perhaps this is what made God angry? Nevertheless, when Adam found out he was going to have to answer for his decision, he blamed the woman. Because the construction of sex as a sin exists, all kinds of pathologies have resulted, including framing African American women as the culprits that lead men astray. You must remember that the Bible was written by some of those same men who were supporting African enslavement in the New World.

I cannot speak for all African American women partly because I am only one of millions of us and because not all African American women have had experiences like mine. I can speak for some African American women though. I have experienced the ills many of us know too well and do not want to speak about. Problems within the family structure, the church structure, and the politics of black thought. Institutionalized issues that are difficult to cut through. I have experienced public patriarchy through the denial of career opportunities because of the combination of my race and gender in spite of my abilities and qualifications. I have watched the waves of society capture black boys and felt the lack of power to do anything about it. I have been called uppity by a Euro American man who was my boss when I sought to live my life to the fullest and for whom I made millions of dollars and who sought "to console" me during the LA riots over Rodney King. And I have experienced the unintended effects of patriarchy by men who have no idea that they are programmed to operate with such a mentality—had a Euro American man working in a coffee shop lay my change on the counter because he did not want to touch me; been denied national funding for my academic projects; been offered solicitations for sex in exchange for an academic placement; experienced being denied contracts and most importantly experienced racism from Euro American academic women.

I'm a Man.
You aint shit.
Aint I a Woman?
Fuck you bitch.

Opening Moves

This chapter first marries and then divorces hip hop dance from patriarchy. It theorizes how the text speaks a historical story of equitableness between African American men and women. It also shows how the danced text tells us that the black man is powerful and power seeking, while at the same time arguing that the black woman's matriarchy is a myth. An African American comedian can help get me started.

Comedian Chris Rock says in one of his comedy routines (HBO Home Video, 1999) that men want three things from women: to be fed, to be attended to sexually, and for women to be quiet. The way he sets the audience up, mostly African American men and women, to hear the requirements, and his actual words yield huge amounts of laughter. It really is not funny but the joke attests to some of the beliefs that support and perpetuate hegemonic patriarchy as does the majority of African American male rap music played in mainstream media. The system of patriarchy is a construction supporting capitalism, a construction made to look as if it were a "natural" arrangement of society. Problems in and amongst African America, not the least of which are sexism, sexual exploitation and gender discrimination hiding behind the all oppressive elements of racism, show themselves in hip hop dance. In this chapter I subject the text to my feminist evaluation.

We have to have our own definition of what it means to be men and women. Chris Rock's statement about how he likes women to behave may not be a true depiction of how all men perceive women, but it serves to reinforce a negative place in the social fabric for women in general, and a disconnect between African American men and women specifically. Chris Rock wants the roles of African American men and women to seem as though they are natural, as if they were puritan and Christian, instinctual and normal, as if coded in the DNA. This is not really different from John Gray's (1992) work of Venus and Mars. Gray reinforced the so-called natural differences in the way men and women think, the way they process information and the way each of us likes to be treated. The differences between men and women have nothing

81

to do with how we treat each other, and certainly do not support sexism, sexual exploitation, and gender discrimination.

Gray is not the only author to have placed the "natural" differences of women and men in mainstream consumption. Patricia Allen's (PhD) 1995 *Getting to I Do* encourages the reader to understand the "natural" differences between male and female energies. She suggests that the person possessing the male energy "naturally" plays the dominant role in relationships. She cleverly avoids alienating alternative lifestyle relationships by saying anyone can be the male energy by choice but both partners cannot both be one or the other at the same time. Nevertheless it is the male energy that has the "natural" tendency to drive, earn large sums of money, make decisions, be respected, generate ideas. The "natural" tendency for the feminine energy is to be passive, soft, waiting, careful with her mouth, cherished and nurtured. These "natural" feminine energy characteristics will eventually transform the masculine energy into being more responsible and minimize the male energy's tendency toward sexual exploitation and selfishness.

Iyanla Vanzant's most recent book, *Up From Here: Reclaiming the Male Spirit,* was the subject of a talk she gave in June 2002 at a church in Los Angeles. I have to say that I have enjoyed many of her books and appreciate the contribution she has made to African American spirituality. However, at that talk, one of the behaviors she admonished women to pay attention to was the way they talk to men, to "mind your mouth" because men cannot, as I interpret it, "naturally" keep up with what you are saying, and they cannot process information as well as women can. Moreover, women should not be demanding in relationships with men. That men "naturally" want to be protectors, providers, performers and pleasers, but they are terrified of what women say and what other men will think of them because our society has not provided a place for men to express their emotions without being ridiculed. I agree with Vanzant's assessment of the societal lack of support for men's, particularly African American men's, emotional health. I do not agree that there is a natural relationship between what African American women say with their mouths and bodies and whether men can or cannot express their emotions that supports sexism and gender discrimination. On the contrary, if anything we need to continue to open our mouths and talk about how sexism and gender discrimination handicaps our functioning and how we like to ignore that fact with building solidarity to combat racism.

The system of patriarchy that has seduced African American men into believing they can dominate and abuse women — sexually, mentally, emotionally, economically — and that has lured African American women into believing that a man should naturally protect and provide for them needs to be taken out with a few AK-47s and some 9 millimeter semi-automatics. We need to understand that being "down for the cause of racism" is not a substitute or a reason to gloss over sexism and gender discrimination amongst African Americans. Removal of patriarchy requires development of a system to replace it, and before that it must be realized that the game is not about being like Euro Americans. That means we have to talk to each other as individuals and honestly recognize and acknowledge which belief systems we chose to operate under.

Each of us, if we choose belief systems knowledgably, can figure out what we want for our lives separate and apart from prevailing ideologies of Euro American success. That type of success being defined as achieving the American dream which includes, for a man, having a woman you can control and earning money in the cut-throat throes of capitalism. For a woman it means "minding her mouth," having babies, putting her goals and aspirations on the back burner so her man can pursue cut-throat capitalism, and being dependent on him to be a protector, provider, pleaser and performer, roles he is apparently afraid of (Vanzant 2002).

African American male rap songs found in underground market circulation go a long way in criticizing racism and often, but not always, avoid perpetuating female exploitation. These rappers understand that they are not being made better by beating or raping women, abandoning their babies, and minimizing women by calling them derogatory names in order to feel powerful or to deal with their "terror" (Vanzant 2002). Unfortunately a large percentage of commercial rap and media driven hip hop dance supports the definition of capitalistic success and the exploitation of women. Hip hop dance disseminated in this manner is a Eurocentric patriarchical depiction of sexism played out on African American bodies.

Largely marginalized, some African American female rap artists, like Queen Latifah, MC Lyte, Lauren Hill, Lil' Kim, TLC, and many others, critically approach problems of sexism and gender discrimination in their lyrics and bodily movements. It seems that they recognize, like many of us should but certain messages hide, that the average African American man usually does have the means and intelligence to take financial responsibility for himself, and the ability to take 100 percent financial responsibility for other people, namely his children. But what about the African American men taking responsibility for African American women? They can do that as well.

Feminist Hip Hop Dance

African American women hip hop dancers (and rappers) deconstruct the notion that the female body should naturally be protected because it is weak, frail and rapable. They posit that they are against living in a state of fear about being raped, a state of being evaluated as second class citizens, or a state of endurance of oppression from sexual exploitation physically, emotionally, materially; that they are independent from patriarchal men and there is nothing but good in that. They can use their bodies as they see fit and not have to mold themselves into an imposed image of femininity. African American male rappers such as Biggie Smalls support this deconstruction when he goes so far as to sum up his song "Sky's the Limit" on his *Life After Death* album (Bad Boy Records, 1997): he wants to make it so that his daughter does not need a man in this sense, and LL Cool J (Columbia Records, 1990) supports this deconstruction in his desire to have "a round the way girl." The "round the way girl" is not afraid to speak her mind, is independent, has a "bad" attitude, and he not only respects her for these attributes but is attracted to her because of them.

It would seem at first glance that African American women were excluded from early forms of hip hop dance in much the same manner that we have been excluded from every other aspect of American society with the exception of sex and labor. Our bodies have been used like those of men in capital formation since we were first transported here. And our bodies have been used as actual sites of sexual abuse and symbols of erotica. We were brought here and made to labor, and part of that labor included satisfying the sexual exploitation of white men. After the so-called emancipation of African Americans, there came a move for (white) women's equality, women's rights and her right to vote. To the chagrin of many a white woman, Euro American men were more open to the idea that African American men should vote before Euro American women did. African American women have lived on the lowest rung of the social totem pole since we arrived here by slave ship centuries ago. Euro Americans reinforced their sexual bias and privilege over African American women through African American men even in slavery. Certain tasks and chores were not available to the African American male slave because of his gender; all tasks were open to the African American woman (hooks 1981).

But on closer inspection, we see that African American women have not been excluded from the formative years of hip hop dance and are not excluded now. As Mimi Valdes states in *Hip Hop Divas,* "[African American] women have been a part of hip hop since day one.... They make music designed to counteract racism and sexism in the music industry and society at large [and female rapper Eve] was busy proving that an MC could tackle serious female issues" (Valdes 2001, x). Similarly, Kierna Mayo contributed a selection about Queen Latifah in *Hip Hop Divas* where Mayo interprets the album cover of Queen Latifah's *All Hail the Queen* as saying "hip hop will forevermore deal with gender as well as race" (Mayo 2001, 53). And let us not forget that rap music was launched through "Rapper's Delight" (Rhino Records, Inc., 1979) by the Sugar Hill Gang, promoted by Sylvia Robinson. African American women have always been a part of hip hop dance but the media focuses so much on men that the women are left out (Harris 2002; Rose 1994).

In reality, the hip hop industry was conceived of by an African American woman. In 1981, Funky 4 + 1 More, led by African American female rapper Sha, was "the first to introduce hip hop to the white media" (Veran 2001, 8) on *Saturday Night Live*. According to *Hip Hop Divas*, during the eight years between 1978 and 1986 more than 60 successful rap records were produced which featured female MCs and DJs. Clearly these statistics indicate that African American women were involved. Moreover, the contributions made were resistive and comprised intellectual productions (Collins 1991). At the same time, new intellectual production came through hip hop dance as well.

African American female rappers eventually got pushed to the back burner. While there were and still are many African American males who were supportive and protective of African American female hip hop artists, the problem was that the machine of Euro American male music production took over, which generally did not and does not deem African American women artists as profitable as their male counterparts. Someone remarked that the culture of hip hop was evolving into the business of rap: a multizillion-dollar commodities market hotter than well-fed pork bellies, and the way of life that evolved from street-speak was moving on up to Wall Street, but African American women rappers were perceived as not as profitable. There are, of course, some African American female rap artists who are extremely wealthy, a result of their actual profitability in the hip hop industry. My point is that hip hop was a joint effort that disjoined when picked up on the capitalist radar screen.

It seems to me that what African American men aspire to have is power. They want some of the power the affluent Euro American man has. Historically, what the African American man saw was a white man who had money at his disposal and whose wife and children and workers and slaves were subject to his domination, you know, like what it says in Genesis. In terms of assimilating into American culture, this was part of the American dream: that a man could invest himself in capitalism and reap financial and social rewards of domination equating to male dignity. Unfortunately reaching this vista remained, and remains in some cases, a far off pipe dream for many African American men. And what does this say for the African American woman? Does she want to be what some authors have described as "chickenheads"? Does she want to be taken care of financially? I think she wants equality for the race as a whole and the total elimination of sexual exploitation.

Not surprisingly then, hip hop dance has been categorized as a man's dance, especially with the advent of break dancing. In reality there were b-girls and b-boys in equal proportions at hip hop dance's inception. These b-girls and b-boys provided the seeds for what we now know as hip hop dance. At a b-boy b-girl session, African American men and women were competing with each other for showmanship and perhaps the respect of their crew, and took the opportunity to write some history. As b-boys' and b-girls' texts were taken up by media-defined break dancing, women were left out of the picture. The sad thing is that the competition for elements of pride and dignity did not translate into the same ideals for African American women. Instead, what was translated was another placement of women into the role of sex object. Mainstream hip hop music video portrays African American women with their breasts and buttocks as commodities, and the relationships between African American women and men as purely antagonistic. The capitalist media machine is doing what has been done for centuries (Collins 2000).

As hip hop dance evolved from break dancing into waack and rap dance, we see the presence of more and more African American women but not because they were not integral to b-girlin. Moreover, a b-girl move is not a sexual representation; more and more women are portrayed on the screen as pure sex objects or as people to be abused physically and emotionally and mentally. This is not new to American culture. Before it hit the media, hip hop dance was not about the sexual exploitation of women. It was about communicating what was going on historically between African Americans and Euro Americans with respect to their exclusion from the capitalist machine. African American men and women, by and large, have been left out and left behind in terms of being able to accumulate wealth in proportion to whites according to standards of capitalism. Many have been brainwashed into believing that the reason they cannot accumulate this wealth is because of the strength and dominance of African American women who will not submit to men as the Euro American woman submits to her man. What this means is that the African American woman has been blamed for the ills of the African American race. And some even believe these accusations. In many hip hop music videos we see the African American woman having sex, being pursued for sex, competing with other women for the prize of the African American man. What African American men are really competing for is a piece — of the wealth they see brandished before them and held ever so tightly by EuroAmerican men.

Hip hop dance then is not a statement by African American men about African American women. It is a historical discussion of the continued exclusion from social interactions that allow for prosperity, wealth, security and power. These are the things that money can buy. But instead, uninformed readers of hip hop dance texts diminish it into something bale, something that once again places African Americans in the limelight of the lowest on the totem pole. About this image, Queen Latifah is quoted in *Hip Hop Divas* as having said, "You have most of the media, which is probably 90 percent controlled by white folks, they give their interpretation of who we are as black people, and all too often you've seen negative images of us" (Mayo 2001, 59). As I have already said, hip hop dance videos are the Euro American male depiction and interpretation of sexism.

Another important aspect of hip hop culture has been the aspect of violence. But one author has noted that the use of the gun in hip hop dance videos is but another phallic symbol. I guess the two sort of look alike. The gun expresses bullets. The penis expresses sperm. The gun is hard. Penises are frequently hard. But a bullet takes life while sperm, united with ova, develop life. So if the gun is a phallic symbol comparable to a penis, it must mean that Euro America thinks that African American penises are deadly. This is not news, of course, as history has shown many African American penises and testicles have been cut off or incarcerated while attached to their bodies, and often for no reason. The portrayal of violence in mainstream hip hop dance video is just another aspect of this old trick of making African American men out to be deadly, uncontrollable, violent sex addicts. But if we look at the types of violent sexual behaviors exhibited by slave owners and slave traders, is not the deadly uncontrollable sex more historically attributable to the Euro American man? Again these images of violence are more about the Euro American man than the African American man. True we do have problems of gangs. But do you think for a moment that if those same gang members were not faced with the totally ridiculous ideology of wanting to be like the Euro American man with limited means of doing so, but rather with hope, support and the knowledge that they could be recognized for their social achievements, that they would be gang members? Hip hop dance expresses the total powerlessness of this dilemma if it is read correctly. It is a question of incommensurability (Tambiah 1979) with respect to reading the codes of the text.

Hip hop dance does discuss sex and sexuality from a different point of view. A popular dance in the early 1980s was The Dog, often danced to George Clinton's "Atomic Dog" (Thump Records, 1993). This is a partner dance that would be categorized as rap dance. Executing the dance correctly involves abdominal and buttocks muscles, a cool facial expression and the ability to improvise. The song lyrics sung by African American men asked the question, "Why do I feel like that why do I chase the cat? Nothin but the dog in me" (Clinton 1993). This was indeed a great song for those of us that danced to, and still dance to, this song whenever we could. But my point is that in doing The Dog, both the African American women and the men were equally responsible for engaging in the dance moves, carrying the cool expression and Signifyin with improvisation. There was no exploitation or sin or badness associated with the text. The text of the dance wrote of the historical celebration of sexuality as a positive virtue between African American women and men and spoke of the ability to withstand racist oppression. Yet elements of this dance have been appropriated into mainstream hip hop dance videos and incorrectly read as vile, dangerous and oppressive sexuality with respect to African American men and at the same time projects African American women as the objects of sexual exploitation.

Hip hop dance overall, I would argue, b-boyin and b-girlin, The Cabbage Patch, The Bounce, The Sea Walk, The Runnin Man, and

The Snake are not only about historical representations of African American men and women in capitalist society having to do with exclusion from means to wealth and security. Some of them can be read as dealing with sexual issues and sexual exploitation. While I have described these dances in earlier chapters, I say again that they reveal ways to handle day to day life in this country from enslavement to the present, and that day to day life includes the African American woman's position as sexual object at the hands of men more powerful than she. Instead of correctly reading these texts, portions of them have been appropriated to sell commodities. In the case of The Dog, it has been appropriated to continue to degrade the sexuality of African American men and women based on Euro American beliefs of original sin.

Bernie Mac, during his introduction in *The Original Kings of Comedy* (MTV Networks, 2000), opens his performance with executing The Dog (no stills are available, as was explained in an earlier chapter). The dance is a greeting to the public. He is fully clothed in a suit and tie and before he opens his mouth, he speaks with his body using the celebratory language of The Dog. He is communicating to his audience, "I'm bad and so are you. I know the struggle still here but look what we doin' anyhow." There is no woman on stage with him. He is dancing alone. This hip hop dance is not about what Euro America has construed it to be. It is not about African American women being uncouth or African American men's penises being the equivalent of a gun or the general picture of vertical intercourse. It is about celebrating heritage, talking of good times, sexual equivalence, and connecting through bodily shared experiences and in a sense Signifyin solidarity amongst African Americans and against the established structures talked about in The Box Step for example. The Box Step is a dance in which the right foot comes across the left and the left foot steps back, and then the right foot steps right. The dance places the speaker in a perpetual box, which indicates being hemmed in, boxed in with nowhere to go. When done in a social setting, this dance can get very funky, as the dancers stoop low and use upper body variations. In this dance very little hip action takes place.

Speaking of signifying, there has been a great deal of rhetoric around the notion of signifying. Authors have written theories about signifying and set up different types of signifying diagrams wherein a word or expression means something that is not actually essential to the meaning given. African Americans have been signifying long before theorists tried to come up with a theory of signification (Gates 1988). What mainstream hip hop dance signifies, that is hip hop dance that is reproduced and appropriated for sale rather than use, is Euro America. Euro America's thinking on everything sexual. Is it not Euro America that uses the camera to show images of sexual abuse of women? Is it not Euro America that sets forth myths and stereotypes about African Americans in general? And is it not Euro America that decides which female rap artists get play? So how did we go from b-boyin and b-girlin on the corner to half naked African American women doing an unintended version of The Dog on mainstream hip hop dance, films and rap videos? Because popular culture is approved by the legal and economic machines, together with educational systems, and these determine which narratives are legitimated and which circulate underground. Government and corporations decide which official interpretations of social reality prevail (Collins 1990, 2006). This is why the images of hip hop dance have degraded to the point that they have.

When you see gyrating hips of semi-nude women in hip hop dance videos, as some would see as a form of sexual exploitation but others see as a form of sexual freedom, think of them as the continued construction of an aspect of capitalism. Sexual exploitation reinforces patriarchal notions embedded in capitalism. Think of gyrating hips, big breasts and exposed abdomens translating into dollars for producers and directors and board members and chairmen of boards, with a few of them trickling down to the dancers. Think of how they help themselves to the aspects of art forms they can cabbage to make a profit. View the women in these videos as women who may otherwise have to accept a more menial position cleaning or typing or cooking in a cafeteria, or worse, prostitution, in order to support themselves. African American women have historically done work that no one else would do in order to survive and in order to provide for themselves and their families — work that an African American man would not do or was not allowed to do, and certainly work that a Euro American man would not do (hooks 1981). With regard to commercial hip hop dance, in a conversation I had with an African American male hip hop dance choreographer, I asked him what he thought about half-naked women shown doing commercial hip hop dance. He said that if a woman wants to appear half naked on the stage or on television or in a video, so be it. This is acceptable to him and he does not think less of her. But *he* is certainly not going to go on stage in his dance belt, just like *he* is not going to clean someone's house in order to put food on the table. An African American woman will do both.

Of course there is the spoken aspect of mainstream hip hop dance video in which the male MC categorizes women as bitches and whores. There are hundreds of examples of hip hop dance videos to go with these types of lyrics, laced with women with gyrating hips, wet lips, big breasts, hanging out of low rider cars or hanging onto drug dealing gang bangers and pimps. I think we have to face the fact that there is an aspect of our society that likes seeing and hearing these representations of African Americans. As I mentioned earlier in this book, the hip hop dance videos and songs that speak about the political situation and the history of our existence in the United States do not get the same attention as these songs and dances that serve only to undermine, cover and distract from the real issues, issues of poverty, poor quality education, poor or non-existent health care, high mortality rates, sexism, racism, and so on. Remember we are dealing with a capitalist mechanism that seeks both to profit and to sell its hegemonic structure at the same time. It is not likely that sales of underground hip hop dance and music will forward that very narrow and exploitative agenda.

The African American Feminist Agenda in Brief

Support for the African American feminist agenda can be found in hip hop dance. As I interpret it, there are several items on that agenda to be reckoned with. One is the cessation of misogynistic patriarchal practices. Another is the cessation of racist practices. The third is the cessation of the practice of racism as a cover to sexism. Fourth is for African Americans to stop buying into the sexism and racism of capitalism. And finally a complete end to the idea that the successful achievement of agenda items one through four will some how make men powerless beings.

Uncommercialized hip hop dance has never set forth misogynistic practices portraying men hating women. The dances are not like ballet where men and women have particular roles to play on a stage and men are dominant while women are weak. They are social dances that set up the partners as equal and valuable in their own right. Even hip hop dance that is staged often shows African American men and women performing the same movement vocabulary. It is not set up to portray, as in ballet or baroque, African American women as weak, or to show African American men as dominant. In hip hop dance clubs, those that are frequented predominately by African Americans, the rules of etiquette go like this. If you want to dance, you dance. African American women and men are free to engage in bilateral dance invitations. This is certainly true for house dances.

On the other hand, commercialized hip hop dance often does engage in portraits of patriarchal misogyny, although at first glance you may not see it. Take for example the scene in *Soul Food* (20th Century–Fox Films 1997) where homeboy busts a move on his old flame at his wedding where he is marrying someone else. Since he is marrying someone else it is clear that something went wrong, at some point before the wedding, with the ex-hootchie mama who he's dancing with while his wife — not a hootchie mama — is in the bathroom. They make a scene on the dance floor with their bumping and grinding and homeboy is gettin' off, according to the camera's eye. All the males, from elementary school aged to the old reverend, stop what they are doing to watch the two, but none of them stop the couple from their lewd dancing.

Then the wife gets accosted by her ex — a man whose character represents everything criminally powerful — with an open invitation to engage in sex since he is convinced that she did not know what she was doing when she chose to marry her husband, who is totally absorbed by the devil in a short blue dress on the dance floor. Both African American male characters in this scene ignore the person embodied in the African American females they encounter, the choices those bodies have made about them, and these aspects of disrespect and invisibility points up their dislike for them as well. The African American male onlookers co-sign. These messages are transmitted through the context of a dance, an appropriated hip hop dance being performed at a wedding, and are exactly the type of messages the African American feminist agenda wants to address.

As another aspect of that agenda, hip hop dance can be utilized to further attack racism. More people are doing hip hop dance than you can believe. In multiracial hip hop dance clubs, while the tendency is for certain groups to congregate together inside the club, it is not uncommon to see different ethnic groups communicating with each other through dance. By performing the social dances of hip hop they are learning African American history, even if it is unbeknownst to them. This is not to say that I am supporting the multicultural agenda of capitalists and politicians for economic gain. Not at all. I am merely saying that through this genre of dance, people can discuss racist practices without violent or deathly reprisal. This was one of the bases for the development of b-girlin and b-boyin, the precursor to hip hop dance: find a way to discuss the effects of racism and come up with some moves to go forward with based on mutual respect and dignity. In terms of dealing with racist practices between Euro- and African America though, other than documenting the effects of those practices, hip hop dance has so far not established a sustained change in the direction of elimination of racism. It could, however, if the meanings of the dances were read correctly.

Back in the day when the issue of women's suffrage was on the table, Euro American women did not pretend not to be racist. They were racist and it came out big time; when they found out that their Euro American husbands would be more willing to grant African American men the right to vote, they were furious. Their fury unveiled the racism against African American women that they so desperately tried to hide and deny. At the same time, and even as African American women established their own beneficial women's groups, African American women sought to align themselves with African American men to fight racism, and often to their detriment through the silencing and ignoring of sexism. Of course, racism has been a cover for sexism for centuries. Sexism comes in many different shapes, sizes and colors (pardon the pun on penises). But simply stated sexism is the denial of a person's selfhood, sexuality, choices, economic gain and personal development by virtue of the possession of particular genitals. Hip hop dances like The Snake and The Cabbage Patch are commentaries on the capitalist society that constructs sexism as a constraint to access to certain choices, economic gains and personal development that define selfhood and chosen sexuality.

One practice that could go a long way towards achieving one of the African American feminist agenda items would be to have African Americans stop buying into the messages set forth that would have us continue to think negatively about ourselves, our bodies, our heritage, our language, our dancing, our abilities, our men and our women. For whatever set of reasons and circumstances, the reality is that African American women have worked, and not infrequently, to support men. It is not because we are matriarchs or that we are domineering over men, or that we all think our men are no good. It is because we have had to work. The reality is that African American men work too. And here's a news flash: many of them do not think of the women in their lives as bitches and whores. Now this is not to say that there are not any bitches and whores or woman-haters or no-good men; there are. But the fact of the matter is that bitches and whores and no-good men are found in many cultures. African American people are attractive, intelligent, entrepreneurial, responsible, creative, diligent, literate, literary, inventive, loving, kind, giving, helpful. All of these attributes show up in African American culture, contributing to American culture and its success, and especially in hip hop dance.

African American feminists are not at odds with African American men inasmuch as the agenda is not one that seeks to castrate, render them powerless, demean or destroy. Actually the agenda is empowering. This is not to say that there are not some horribly sexist

African American men, even men who would deny being sexist as an African American woman brings him dinner with a blackened eye he gave her. By the same token, there are some African American women who are whores, who do not know who the baby's father is, who want to be taken care of financially, generally hate men, *et cetera*. But the overriding message that we take in year after year is that *all* African American women are whores or castrators, and *all* African American men are women abusers, and that *all* African American men are against African American feminism. This is simply not true. Hip hop dance text lets us see these and other truths in the way in which it is performed equally, allowing both genders to write valuable historical documents, and theorize our positionality within American capitalism. It also gives space for theorizing relationships between African American men and women within the sexist and racial structures existing in America for centuries.

Trick Turned

As stated earlier in this chapter, it has been an institutionalized American assumption that African American men have historically been denied certain access to power and wealth and therefore cannot easily support women and children as white men do. Statistics will be presented later on that challenges whether this assumption is still true, an assumption so many of us have bought lock, stock and barrel. I know I did. While looking at those statistics, I also want to revisit some of those I presented in previous chapters. But first, in *On Our Own Terms — Race, Class, and Gender in the Lives of African American Women*, written in 1997 by Leith Mullings, I found some statistics that made my head swim. Did you know that most white men cannot support their own families alone? The white woman has to work. Believing in the myth that a man should be the sole provider for his family is detrimental. Did you know that the myth of the nuclear family has kept many in bondage for years? For the most part, it does not exist. Most homes are not comprised of a man, woman and two children and a dog, all surrounded by a picket fence. Did you know that American images of what a woman should be (stay at home, care for her family, be available for her man, be fragile, etc.) apply only to such a small percentage of white women that you would be embarrassed to admit you believed in that image? I am. Did you know that this small percentage of frail and fragile women who form the basis of the hegemonic position of women also got put into the Bible and sets up how relationships are to be and therefore makes it seem natural? And most of the trouble between African American men and women originates in this myth? In other words, the so called problem between African American men and women is made up, a myth, a lie, a foundationless pit of rhetoric that so many of us have believed for so long. I did.

All of these myths and lies are put into place to make the capitalistic society function. You are just a cog in its wheel. You have been since the first Africans were enslaved and brought over. And the manufactured problems between African American males and females are just another cog. More importantly, sexism is a cog in that wheel and the African American man has bought into that too out of sheer ignorance. The messages of hip hop dance do not support mythology. They are against being bamboozled. They support reality, intellectualize experiences and give directions in which to move to avoid being tricked into believing the hype. Contrary to historical positions and the beliefs of many, what African Americans have to say and what we think is important. We need to write and live our own reality. And that is what we have been doing through hip hop dance. Many of us do not have private capital and are exploited through public capital. Hip hop dance is not counted as any kind of asset; you cannot find it on any balance sheet or income statement. But you should be able to. You cannot write any company or individual and ask for permission to use it. You should be able to. It is exploited through public capital and shows up on balance sheets and income statements disguised as increased sales of all manner of other products.

African American women in hip hop dance videos and film are examples of the backlash described by scholar and feminist Susan Faludi's 1991 *Backlash: The Undeclared War Against American Women.* Her book is representative of the progress feminism has made to bridge

Table 3-1. Translating Hip Hop Labor*

Number of People over 16 with Jobs

African Americans	16,000,000		African Americans living in the US
Non–Hispanic Whites	102,000,000		Non–Hispanic Whites living in the US
Total	118,000,000		

Total Population

35,100,000	12% of all jobs
193,000,000	74% of all jobs
228,100,000	

Percent of People over 16 with Jobs

Men, African American	65.90%	of African American men over 16 in labor force, or 6,422,740 total.
Men, Non–Hispanic White	74.30%	of Non–Hispanic White men over 16 in labor force.
Women, African American	63.40%	of African American women over 16 in labor force, or 7,871,093 total.
Women, Non–Hispanic White	60.30%	of Non–Hispanic White women over 16 in labor force.

Unemployed Labor Force (People over 16 without jobs), 1999

Men, African American	9.20%	of African American men over 16 unemployed, or 896,650 total.
Men, Non–Hispanic White	3.90%	of Non–Hispanic White men over 16 unemployed.
Women, African American	8.50%	of African American women over 16 unemployed, or 1,055,273 total.
Women, Non–Hispanic White	3.30%	of Non–Hispanic white women over 16 unemployed.

*Notes:

Source: US Census Bureau, 1999.

As of the date of this report, there were 16 million African Americans and 102 million Non–Hispanic Whites who were 16 years old or older in the labor force.

Only African Americans and Non–Hispanic Whites are considered; therefore the numbers do not add up to 100.

Keep in mind that unemployment and labor figures measure only people who report themselves as such.

Jobs are not counted based on wages or salary; African Americans have mostly lower paying and non-managerial positions and these positions could be part-time as well.

The numbers of African American men and women employed and unemployed were calculated by using the US Census data for categories of African American people over 18 years old, so they do not add up to the total number of African Americans with jobs over 16 years of age, and are therefore off by 10%. The data was manipulated only to show a rough estimate of the numbers of African Americans with or without jobs by gender.

Table 3-2. Translating Hip Hop Income*

Family Income	African-American Married	African-American Female only	African-American Male only
Less than $25,000	21%	67%	43%
$25,000 to $34,999	13%	13%	19%
$35,000 to $49,999	18%	11%	17%
$50,000 to $74,999	25%	7%	15%
$75,000 and over	23%	3%	7%

Family Income less than $25,000

	Less than $25,000	
African American families with no man	67%	41% (below poverty level)
Non-Hispanic White families with no man	46%	21% (below poverty level)
African American families with no woman	43%	20% (below poverty level)
Non-Hispanic White families with no woman	26%	8% (below poverty level)

People in Poverty in the US

African Americans	9,100,000	(out of total 35,100,000)
Non-Hispanic Whites	15,800,000	(out of total 193,000,000)

Children in Poverty in the US
African American	37%
Non-Hispanic Whites	11%

Elders in Poverty in the US
African Americans	26%
Non-Hispanic Whites	8%

Men in Poverty in the US
African American	23%
Non-Hispanic Whites	7%

Women in Poverty in the US
African American	29%
Non-Hispanic Whites	9%

*Notes:
Source: US Census Bureau, 1999.
Poverty level is $16,000 yearly income for a family of 4.

the gap between it and African American feminism, and it also points out very clearly the extent to which myths are perpetuated between men and women to squelch attempts to eliminate sexist practices. A suggestion would be that before you buy into any ideas about what is going on in the African American community or what is going on with

Table 3-3. Translating Hip Hop Business Ownership*

Non-Hispanic white men Own 85% of US businesses
and Take 93% of All receipts.

	Number of Firms	Sales Millions of $	Sales, %
All US Firms	20,821,934	18,553,243	n/a
African American	823,499	71,215	4.00
Men	443,643	51,069	less than 1
Women	312,884	13,551	less than 1
Equally Owned	66,972	6,595	less than 1

African American Firms by Industry Type

Services, 52%
Non-Classified Industry, 12%
Retail Trade, 11%
Transportation, Communication, Utilities, 9%
Construction, 7%
Finance, Insurance, Real Estate, 5%
Agriculture, 2%
Manufacturing, Wholesale Trade, 1% each

*Notes
Source: US Census Bureau, 1997.
Firms having more than $1,000 in receipts reported in 1997 income tax returns are
counted as firms.

African American women and men, you check the statistics yourself.
Anything that is said enough times can be made to seem true (Faludi
1991). The media and American social institutions have taken what we
find sacred, namely our dance, and turned it into a capitalistic enterprise whose sole aim has been to provide continued controlling images
of African Americans, a backlash in its own right to mask both sexism
and racism.

But even with the controlling images, the business sector recognizes the ability of attaching hip hop dance to products not associated
with African Americans, which in and of itself continues the reinforcement of the control. The machine of capitalism cannot resist the call
of the market. This can be acknowledged if it is recognized that the
capitalist agenda against the black feminist agenda has been established
by influential and affluent men, mainly to date, white. These men are

the leaders of media, business, educational and political mechanisms. What can be twisted for profit and control will be. Let us see what their agenda is trying to hide. We can do The Cabbage Patch now, or we could do The Runnin Man or The Bounce, and certainly The Box Step; we need to bring in The Crip Walk; we will certainly want to write something after we read the statistics in Tables 3-1, 3-2, and 3-3.

Table 3-1—Translating Hip Hop Labor is a summary of findings reported recently by the US Census Bureau. It is broken down into categories of people with jobs who are over 16 years old as compared with Euro American counterparts. The statistics are placed together with those of EuroAmericans because the data often hides important information. For example, of the unemployed labor force, the data presented by the US Census Bureau makes it look like African American men have a higher unemployment rate than African American women. That is true proportionately because there are more African American women than men. The data show that 9.20 percent of African American men are unemployed, while only 8.50 percent of African American women are. These statistics are sad when compared to the unemployment rate of Euro Americans; we are unemployed and underemployed by twice the rate of whites. But what is hidden is that there are more African American women unemployed when compared to the men, equating to about the same number of African American men in prison.

Let us turn to Table 3-2 — Translating Hip Hop Income. More African American women live in poverty than African American men. African American families led by women make up 67 percent of our households, and 59 percent of them live above the poverty level which is defined as $16,000 (this is still poverty) for a family of four. Looking at the 43 percent of African American men who lead households without a woman on the other hand, 80 percent of them live above the poverty level. Nearly 98 percent of all households headed by African American women earn less than $75,000 per year while 92 percent of African American men who head households without women earn less than $75,000 per year. Both of these are sad commentaries assuredly about how few of us earn more than $75,000 per year, but the point is that African American men are somewhat better off. In every income category which he heads, African American male income fares better than those same categories of African American women. Seventy-seven percent of married African American couples find themselves earning less than $75,000 per year, but the majority of them fall in the $50,000 to $74,999 range. It is difficult to say whether married couples are better off than unmarried African American couples because we cannot say for certain how many people a couple's income supports. However, it is noteworthy that in each of the first three income categories, African American men without women do better percentage wise than either married couples or African American women who head households. To earn higher levels of income it seems as though the message is that one must be married. Summarizing aspects of African American income, we have nearly one-third of all African Americans living in poverty, including 37 percent of our children, 26 percent of our elderly, 29 percent of our women and 23 percent of our men.

In terms of business ownership, Table 3-3 presents information relative to the United States. African Americans own firms that represent a measly 4 percent of all US sales but that equate to over $71 million in annual sales. More than half of them are owned by African American men who make approximately $51 million in annual sales, while in the neighborhood of 37 percent of African American firms owned by African American women make $13.5 million in annual sales. The US Census Bureau reports that over half of all African American firms are of the services sector and the remaining are in decreasing proportions distributed over retail trade, communication, construction, real estate, agriculture and manufacturing.

African American men are doing better economically, even with prison terms, according to the most recent reports by the US Census Bureau, than African American women, children and elderly. When did that happen? That is not the message we get! I have not been getting it, have you? Is that a result of adaptation of Euro American methods of patriarchy and domination or so-called African American women matriarchs? US Census Bureau data show that African American men, on average, have been earning significantly more than African American women in every age group, education attainment level and nearly every occupation for a long time. It follows logically then, as validated in a report issued in 1994 by the US Department of Commerce, that the median incomes for African American men outpace those of African American women by significant margins.

How do these statistics compare to historical representations of Africans? In describing relationships between men and women in pre–European slavery in Africa, Mullings says

> it is probable that in many of the societies from which slaves were removed, the definition of masculinity was not based on the [economic] dependence of women, that men and women frequently had independent arenas and occupations, and that men and women had asymmetrical but not necessarily unequal roles [Mullings 1997, 82].

The statistics show that unequal roles do exist for African American adults amongst themselves based on concepts of domination of women. As a side comment, we should keep in mind that Africans had a part to play in the way slavery impacted the world. I can imagine the answer an African woman would have given to a European male inquiring about purchasing people for enslavement on other continents. Her answer would probably have been a resounding "NO." I know African women were involved in slave trading too, but to a lesser degree than African men. None of this is to imply an origin for the "natural" relationship between African American men and women or blame African men for enslavement. No, simply that statistics can be made to show what people want to show. Most important, we cannot continue to believe that the problems of African America rest on the African American woman's ways of thinking and being. We are not effeminizing African American men — Euro America wants us to believe we are — or hos or bitches or sapphires or workhorses or work oxen or baby machines.

What is called motherhood for Euro American women is called sexual looseness and promiscuity for African American women. All of that is a constructed social myth that operates in the wheel of capitalism. Hip hop dance, when writing about experiences and deconstructing the beliefs of the dominant does not position women in these boxes, but The Box Step gives African American women a way to theorize and write about it. It also does not position men as shiftless, no-good, or sex addicts that you have to run from; but The Box Step gives African American men a way to theorize and write about it. What is called masculine for Euro American men is made to be feared when seen in African American men. What is seen as patriarchal sexism in Euro American men is labeled criminal behavior in African American men.

What is natural? The color of grass is natural; that the sun rises every day is natural. That people eat, sleep, procreate and eliminate is natural. Women have vaginas and men have penises. That is natural (usually). But it is not natural that hip hop dance signifies promiscuous African American women and misogynistic, narcissistic, sex addicted African American men. The construction of these images on the screen has a particular purpose which is not the same purpose of the danced text. Hip hop dance provides an interpretation of meanings.

Synthesizer

African American feminist thought is complicated by many factors, and I do not profess to know all of them. But a few have informed this writing. First you have the whole issue of feminism defined by Euro Americans, which to my understanding has historically been about finding a place of equality for oppressed middle class women. Then you have the problem of Euro American women who are not middle class who were excluded from that prevailing feminist ideology in general. And finally you have African American women who have been caught between what Euro American feminism says it is and the African American woman's lived experience with Euro American women's discrimination against them.

It is precisely because of African American women's experiences that make the language and text of hip hop dance so important. The text of hip hop dance is also important for African American men. Only there, composing the choreography of the social dance, could we write what happened to us, why we think it did, and what message to send to readers. It is because of that writing that I am able to write this book. Hip hop dance is not about getting away from sexism, racism or class hierarchies. It is about acknowledging them and commenting on them, as well as documenting and historically solving them. Each dancer writes of individual experiences in the journal of resistance. African American feminist thought written in hip hop dance encourages self-esteem, the questioning of knowledge structures and sources, and building of bonds that foster forward movement. That encouragement of collective identity, self-esteem and self-knowledge applies equally to African American men penciling out their names in The Crip Walk, being tactical with writing The Pop Lock — popping the proverbial locks on chains either real, mythical, or imagined — and speaking about his worth by referencing The Dog before he addresses a crowd.

Hip hop dance offers this same identity and view Collins (1991) speaks about, along with confidence in African American subjective knowledge bases. Hip hop dance is a way for oppressed African Americans to either develop or maintain their shreds of confidence, to theorize about their experiences and position within a social structure and to encourage collective understanding of the ills that confront them. It is a way for African American women to theorize about how she knows — without seeing statistics — the unfairness of her being paid less than an African American man in the same job even as she put the sexist agenda item second in order to fight against racism. This is why seeing a commercial featuring a glass bottle decorated with frizzy hair, sunglasses, baggy clothes and gold chains mimicking break dancing to sell Snapple juice products on national television is pathetic. None of our theoretical writings are understood in degenerate portrayals of hip hop dance on bodies or inanimate objects, placed there by people of, as anthropologist Stanley J. Tambiah had defined it, incommensurate experience or by downright disrespect.

None of what I have written here is meant to deny that we have problems between African American men and women. But as I have said earlier, those to me are only resolved when we understand that the conflicts between African American men and women are part of the machinery of our society. I recommend we continue to theorize, since we know that when an African American rapper says something about a bitch or a whore, he is not talking about me or you and when an African American woman hip hop singer is saying "niggahs ain't shit," she is talking about her experience and not all men. Hip hop dance as text does not operate in the phallocentric, phallogic, and logocentric masculine economy. It does not operate within the "competitive, atomistic liberal individualism" of Euro American feminism. Hip hop dances as commodities do operate in these spheres. But this is not a theory I have to point out to some of you.

The game of patriarchy, the Euro American game, is one where goods and services are exchanged for money and security. Euro American women allegedly get money and security in exchange for giving sex and deferring their brains, opinions and observations to their man. Historically, African Americans have aspired to play this game, but the problem we are told is that African American men have been denied access to money with which to play the game. When they do get it, according to data given from the US Census Bureau, they are unwilling to exchange it with others in their community, namely African American women and children — the people Vanzant (2002) and Allen (1996) say men "naturally" want to protect, provide, perform for and please. Perhaps African American women have been labeled for so long as not being valuable enough to make such an exchange with in the first place, but rather need to be pimped, or that African Americans do not need each other, that we African Americans all believe this lie. That is, the lie that African American men have been denied access to money with which to play the game of patriarchy, that they are all in prison, on drugs, pimping, etc., and that they have less money than African American women and that all of this is her fault since she is a matriarch on the one hand, and the biblical cause of the fall of man on the other.

Hip hop dance when commoditized and positioned in the broader economy can be seen as a currency that women use to exchange goods and services for money. In the separate economy of written text, hip hop dance does not function this way. It provides instead use value that enables the writers and readers of the dance — who know how to interpret it — historical information and commentary about the state of affairs in the United States. This information and commentary includes mirrors that reflect Eurocentric patriarchy, racism and sexism situated in a capitalistic economy. Moreover, the hip hop dance text mirror I am speaking of reflects the lived experience, the known impossibility of fully assimilating into the state of affairs, and rejects hierarchal relationship patterns so prevalent in Euro American institutions.

There are African Americans that practice hip hop dance as text, and there are African American persons who practice hip hop dance as commodity, and the practices are not always mutually exclusive. What I want to avoid and what I want readers to take away from this is that the essentializing of hip hop dance and hip hop music to either bitches and hos, or niggahs and gangstas, is unacceptable. The separation and delineation of roles for African American men and women as understood and enacted by Euro American society do not apply to hip hop dance as text. Both African American men and women write hip hop dance texts, just as both African American men and women rap. The notion of categorizing one or the other comes from a Western ideology which is overlaid on everything Euro America sees.

PART II

HIP HOP APPROPRIATION

4

Theorizing Hip Hop Dance Consumption

"But the bar for authentic participation in the American experience that generates hip hop culture is much higher than it was, say for a white jazz musician in the 1950s. The majority of the audience — the white majority — demands it."

— Leon E. Wynter,
American Skin, 2002, 37

"The language of the streets is becoming the language of Madison Avenue, as advertising slogans veer toward the vernacular.... One reason for adopting the vernacular [is that it] enables advertisers to co-opt popular phrases."

— Leon E. Wynter (2002, 127) quoting
Stuart Elliot, "Gotta Talk Like This,
It's a Reflection of Buyers' Speech,"
New York Times, March 9, 2002

In the previous chapters, we have seen hip hop dance as a Diaspora related movement. It has been theorized and re-viewed from a feminist perspective. In so doing, several ads have been referenced in the course of this book where hip hop dance was used as an attention getting vehicle: Pepto-Bismol, Jell-O Pudding, and JC Penney to name a few. Why has hip hop dance been used in this way? It has to do with several factors. They include the browning of America in pursuit of profits by corporations and at the same time reduction of tensions between ethnic minorities and dominant cultures. The browning is intimately integrated with Green Americans, layered upon the notion, the false notion, that an individual can construct a self identity that he so chooses. (As an aside, let me ask rhetorically what identity exactly is up for grabs? Mine is always black and female.) The interstices of these different manipulations serve as the foundation for the new American Dream and are delivered through advertising.

And while that is so, no manipulation can occur where there is resistance or the belief that collective effort can make sweeping changes in the power structure. Hip hop dance was for a flash a pulling down of that power into resistive structures, based on an *emic* understood by those who spoke the language. As has been shown in countless historical tragedies where blacks were perceived as a threat to the American dream, undermining the power structure signified trouble for the capitalist engine. As such, the dance was taken into *etic* forms and linked with products and social identities, giving people the idea that they could be resistive and that this was cool when channeled into consumption. That certainly was a beguiling and seductive rubric and a twisting of cultural differences. Simultaneously it diffused any power that black people may have gained in the process of writing hip hop dance *emic*.

What I would like to do in this chapter now is to talk about the consumption process, explore the ways in which marketing creates and fills needs, and how consumption is connected with identity, itself something that consumers try to simultaneously construct for themselves and emancipate themselves from but fail to do. After I do that I would like to explore how hip hop dance is placed within the consumption framework so that it works to support what I have termed the new American Dream. That dream consists of colorlessness, erasure of any kind of acknowledgement of oppression, and the export of this dream to other countries for the purpose of accumulation. To accomplish these several tasks, I will provide a bit of a summary of some relevant literature. Please do note though that there is a good deal of literature available on the topic of advertising, global marketing, and the way identity is constructed. The scope of this work draws on only a portion of it. Of course there is little if any discussion on the role that hip hop dance has played in this arena; a few texts are available that talk about the use of blackness to fulfill the distribution of colorlessness.

The Consumption Process

Advertising has been around so long it seems like it is a natural phenomenon. In reality, as it is experienced today, it is only about as old as abolition and Reconstruction (Stole 2001, 84). In its infancy, advertising was used to inform consumers about product attributes, and then later in the 1920s it became more systematic in its approaches and goals to develop brand loyalty. More recently, advertising's reason for being is to aid companies to position their brands through social and moral ideals, what has been termed a modern paradigm of abstraction and cultural engineering (Holt 2002). As such, by 2000, expenditures on advertising exceeded $230 billion, representing about 2 percent of the Gross Domestic Product, with the average person in the United States being exposed to 3,000 ads per day (Stole 2001). Large conglomerate and powerful companies need to reach consumers partly because there is intense competition: little difference exists between many consumer products and services so companies are interested in fostering brand loyalty and protecting market share. And consumers are reached through media, paid for by the companies such that media is driven by producers of goods and services.[1] Firms engage in the marketing concept, that is, a philosophy that is supposedly geared to producing only what consumers want. Therefore, consumers are studied intensely in the marketing discipline for clues as to how to get them to buy, keep buying, and buy more.

Consumers are thought to have an array of needs that they try to have filled by consumption.[2] On the other hand, they are said to be defined by every item, not a few, but every item that they consume. Each item fills a need that is connected with the consumer's identity. People and organizations that buy goods and services are divided into camps when they are analyzed in the consumption process. Concerned here with individual consumption, some are said to be more emotional in their decision making while others are termed more rational. The truth is that most people utilize a mixture of both. However, emotions play a strong role in consumption. Moreover, consumption is bifurcated into low and high involvement purchasing decisions, which relate to a number of factors associated with financial, psychological, and social risks.[3] These factors are taken into account when marketers design advertisements and when cues are imbedded into them.

Marketers not only use the marketing concept as a way to approach consumers but they also want to manipulate attitude change and formation. The Elaboration Likelihood Model of consumption is concerned with this at the level of involvement and assumes that attitude change through persuasion occurs in consumers depending on the degree of probability that consumers engage in the advertising message while exposed to an ad.[4] If the probability is low, the peripheral route to persuasion should be used and if it is high, then the central route should be used. Elaboration has everything to do with whether or not people see the ad as relevant to them and their needs. If a product or service is considered important by an individual, then that person will take the time to think about the product's value and attributes, and the ad should be geared for high involvement (attitudes then behaviors).[5] People think then act. On the other hand, if a consumer considers the product or service as important perhaps but not needing extensive cognitive processing, the advertiser needs to gear the message for low involvement (behaviors then attitudes). People do not think; they merely accept or reject the message (Petty *et al.* 1983). The type of ad that one develops depends on the audience being targeted, the product or service being discussed, situational contexts, and where the buyers are in the consumption process, and needs hierarchy.[6]

The steps in the consumer decision purchase process include recognition of a problem, information gathering, selection of alternatives, purchase, and post purchase behavior.[7] Problem recognition can be stimulated by a real or non-real situation. For example, suppose you have a digestion problem. You may ask your spouse or parent or good friend what they think you should do about it. They will ask you some questions and say you need a digestive aid of some type. You search your memory of brands and narrow that down to a set that you would be willing to buy. This is your evoked set. After you have gathered all the information from internal and external sources and developed your evoked set, you determine to go to the all night drugstore open up on the corner. Now you are at a point of purchase. You are standing in the relevant aisle containing all the related medications. At that point in time is when the advertisers for Pepto-Bismol will want you to remember their advertisement, with the characters doing hip hop dance as a cue. Purchasing this product is what would be called low involvement: there is little financial, social or psychological risk associated with it. Purchasing the product has some emotional tones to it because you want to feel better — and quickly. If the product does not live up to its promise, or does not effect a cure, then you are only out of a few bucks, feeling little cognitive dissonance, and maybe you go to the doctor. The purchase process would start all over again at that point, but then it would likely become a high involvement purchase, that is, consumption of medical services. In any event, the purchase of Pepto-Bismol says something about your identity because there is also a store brand sitting right next to the major brand. You pick Pepto-Bismol because, even while having a bout of diarrhea, your social identity rests in being cool, or a middle class person who can afford the real thing, and you associate that with the brand.[8] This process can be replayed for a number of low involvement items from clothing to mayonnaise.

All of the steps in the consumer decision purchase process are embodied right there at the moment of decision, for a low involvement, real need situation. There are low involvement decisions of non-real need. What is meant by non-real need is a need that has been created solely by the impact of advertising. For example, I do not need to purchase Jell-O Pudding. I could live without it or eat something else. Advertisers want us to think that we have to have this type of pudding to fill a need, such as a need to be a good parent. Purchasing Jell-O Pudding has nothing at all to do with filling a need, nor does the purchase have any relation to The Snake as a hip hop dance. But, it is the association of the identity with being a cool parent which makes you a good parent because your children will be happy, that points to the identity factor. Again, standing in the aisle trying to decide what to buy for the snacks, lunches or whatnot, the consumer has gone through the stages of the process. The less expensive brand will not do at all. And if the children are happy because the pudding was purchased then there will be little cognitive dissonance.

Besides the use of hip hop dance in the advertisements, who are the people in them? In the Pepto-Bismol one, all the men in the ad are dressed in costumes which erase their ethnicity such that real people are not represented. Similarly, in the Jell-O Pudding advertisement, the cow is composed of two people under a tarp, but the people are not shown, only the "cow's" rear end. The representative person is a little boy with straight hair, but he's not black, not Hispanic, not Asian, not Indian, not Native American. He becomes every brown child doing The Snake.

So we see that, from these two examples of low involvement, real and non-real consumption linking hip hop dance — which it is safe to say is classified as a low popular dance form as opposed to ballet, which is classified as a high art form — to the advertisement serves a purpose of creating market segments of people who will consume the product, or people who will at least keep the product in their evoked set of brands when the point of purchase comes about who do not directly associate blackness with it but rather identity lifted from blackness. With the cues given in the advertisements, and with the whitenizing of the dance, the target market can become "everyman" and "every-woman" of a certain income level who buys digestional aids and pudding. The route to persuasion used in these ads is peripheral. That is, the content of the message tends to be non-verbal rather than verbal, requiring little elaboration.

Of course there are high involvement decisions, with real and non-real problems, involving both emotional and rational behaviors. If the car breaks down beyond repair, and the car is needed to facilitate transportation between home, work, school, and so on, then the need is real. The information search begins. Internally from memory, and externally from family, peer groups, and reliable sources, we gather information that will hopefully help us purchase the right car at the right price, but this time we have to make sure that it is the right brand because of what others are going to think of us. Those others include people at work, church, or other social organizations, the children, the family and the spouse, significant other, partner. The purchase of a car can also be linked to being promoted on the job, or even whether we get the job. After the information is gathered an evoked set of brands is established. Depending on our income category, we may look to buy only German cars, or Japanese cars, etc. The decision to buy a vehicle has already been made, it only boils down to which car and for how much. Cognitive dissonance can be substantial because of all the social and economic risks associated with the purchase. By the same token, it is easy to see how a non-real situation can be created in advertisement, for example, when your car is in perfectly good condition but because it is the end of the season close out, the ad encourages you to hurry in for special financing. In any event, there is an emotional investment different from that found with food products and over the counter medications. Hip hop dance is typically not used in commercial advertisements where high involvement purchases are involved, and the route to persuasion tends to be more central.

The foregoing section briefly explained consumption processes, elaboration, and involvement. Hip hop dance more often than not is tattooed onto low involvement products and services. But why is that? In the upcoming sections, advertising, culture and the importance of hip hop dance in the consumption process will be discussed. This dance form is utilized in developing the most important color and ethnicity, i.e., green and transracial, along with the most important market segments and target markets.

Advertising and Black Culture

Frith and Mueller have written *Advertising and Societies: Global Issues* (2003), a text wherein the role of advertising by using cultural influences is examined. These authors walk the reader through globalization arising through colonialism dating back to the 1500s through the early 1900s. They also document the rise of the multinational global corporation as a means to economic expansion due to the shrinking domestic economic base that would not sustain the rate of growth sought by capital. Neither globalization as a trend, nor growth of expenditures for advertising products and services, has been unabated since World War II. Frith and Mueller argue that advertising provides a distorted mirror of society by playing on mostly hedonic consumption, and shapes societies such that ads "transmit values, influence behavior of both individuals and value-forming institutions, and even sway national development policies"(10).[9] The way in which advertisers do this is by using nuances of culture, learned behaviors and ways of being imparted to individuals in societies through education, institutions, families, and so forth.

Culture as a concept is most slippery and difficult to define. For the purposes of this work it is seen as the beliefs, values and norms of a group, but given, dictated, and understood by a group that can perpetuate them. In other words, culture is developed and upheld by a dominant group (Brumbaugh 2002). Those dominant groups contain their own cultures as well as subcultures, that is, groups of people that somehow stand apart from what is defined as dominant. In the United States of course, the dominant culture is white Euro American, having a majority in population, sitting at the heads of major political and social institutions, dictating the religion, and controlling the economy. Subcultures include African American, Asian American, and Hispanic American, to name a few of the well known categories. Theoretically speaking, subcultures are knowledgeable of at least two cultural constructs: the dominant culture and their own. In contrast, it is often the case that the dominant culture knows its own very well and only a few of a subculture's cultural schemas. The knowledge may or may not be correct but they are part of the dominant culture's cultural construct of the particular subculture (Brumbaugh 2002). As noted earlier, Leon E. Wynter has written a book called *American Skin: Pop Culture, Big Business and the End of White America* (2002) in which he states that

> From the start, pop culture has been constructed on the facts as well as white fantasies of nonwhites and their cultural norms. American identity

within the pop culture, history shows, is in large part projected onto the culture at large through certain mass-marketed, commodified projections of nonwhite identity [Wynter 2002, 20].

Often these bytes of information are turned into advertising cues seeking to make linkages between culture and consumption.[10] These are not only aimed at the dominant culture, of course, with the relatively recent phenomenon of marketing to nondominant groups. However, in regard to hip hop dance, the dominant culture watching it advertised and linked to products via hedonics has its schemas, i.e., signfications, activated by providing associative cues, massaging attitudes about a product, and reinforcement of some piece of identity construction.

When developing advertisements aimed at a particular culture or subculture, marketers use elements of culture such as written and spoken language, nonverbal communication methods, and needs and values. Frith and Mueller emphasize the point that it is "impossible to truly understand a culture without understanding its language [and] a language cannot be fully understood outside its cultural context" (2003, 31). At the same time though language is influenced by culture, and the same words in one culture can mean something entirely different in another. The same holds true for nonverbal communication language. Advertising designed this way, then, provides an interpretation of culture when presented in the media. Advertising designs can contain representation of non-dominant subcultures, often referred to as representations of the "other." In many cases racism and stereotypes are perpetuated in advertising.

For example, "Before the civil rights movement of the 1960s blacks were only featured in advertisements in subservient roles such as porters, cooks, and bellhops. This type of stereotyping appeared to be 'common sense' until these representations were questioned by a large enough group of people" (Frith and Mueller 2003, 119). Further, in "1967 only 4 percent of ads showed black models" (Frith and Mueller 2003, 127). By 1984 that percentage grew to 9 percent of ads having blacks in them (Escalas 1994, note 3). However in 1991, the number of black actors in prime time advertisements was at about 19 percent (Whittler and DiMeo 1991). And over the last few decades African

Americans being used in advertisements are looking more and more European in their skin complexion, body, and facial features (Frith and Mueller 2003, 129). Because advertisements can and do play a major role in creating and changing political positions and values, nowadays using African American models that come close to what the dominant culture looks like helps that culture to face the so called other, but still remain scornful and contemptuous of its existence.

Wynter (2002) discussed the "browning" of America and how African American cultural cues are manipulated in achieving that. America is not racially diverse anymore; it is transracial now, Wynter contends. The main method underlying the browning ideology is was already referred to as the Green American; that is, money talks and all else walks as a market segment. Wynter suggests, "We're all the same color to Kmart — green — and the same nationality, American" (Wynter 2002, 5). In this construction used and disseminated in popular culture, white no longer equals American, a construction that has existed for centuries. The new Americans spend money too. And if the focus did not shift to include them the capitalist march would have halted. Billions of dollars are available for extraction from Green Americans, while at the same time untold hours of labor are also up for the taking by the capitalists. Green America is any color, nationality, or gender that will spend money and work for a living.

The cultural portrayals of whites and blacks in advertisements, the stereotypes and conflicts, roles and identities, reach back to centuries. The point has always been to reinforce white supremacy and "while much has changed in 170 years, the pattern of appropriation, exploitation, distortion, and ultimate marginalization of black and other non-white cultures" (Wynter 2002, 23) in support of the cultural message of white supremacy has not. Whites could take whatever they saw fit from the subculture for this purpose and profit from it collectively and individually. And while Wynter (2002) believes that the American landscape is shifting towards a more equitable stance, my opinion is that the marketing of pieces and parts of African American culture supports and reinforces white supremacy. Because while white folks are trying out black for a day, they are becoming transracial but real black people are always already black. Nevertheless, the transracial new American Dream is now for sale. "Transracial America, in the marketplace, is a vision of the American dream in which we are liberated from the politics of race to openly embrace any style, cultural trope, or image of beauty that attracts us regardless of its origin" (Wynter 2002, 135). This fake space of unity is only in the hedonistic reality created by advertising messages taking its pick of African American culture and using it for profit. People who own the means of production and the concentration of wealth do not give a damn about browning or greening. They have the money to drive the advertising engine, and more importantly, they are indifferent to anything that has no bearing on profits, wealth accumulation, surplus value generation, or any other capitalistic endeavor. If the message now is that everybody is brown with green in their pockets and we can use African American hip hop dance as a cue to relate it to low involvement product and service consumption decisions — globally — so be it.

Research up to the 1970s, according to Whittler and DiMeo (1991), indicated that whites' reactions to black actors in advertisements were not as positive as they were to whites in advertisements. These authors undertook to examine the degree of change that may have occurred due to the shift in social tides that passed across the United States during the 1960s and 1970s. They looked at salient racial cues used in advertisements such as voice and body characteristics to determine if whites perceived more or less similarity with blacks. They delineated the groups into high prejudiced and low prejudiced when evaluating their reactions to salient racial cues used in low involvement advertisements. One-third or so of the sample was drawn from the $39,999 annual income level, and women comprised 73 percent of the sample; all participants ranged between 17 and 55 years old. Though the sample was not the best, and research methods in marketing have evolved since that study, the results were that low prejudiced whites identified more, i.e., perceived no difference between themselves and the black actors when those actors promoted low involvement products. High prejudiced whites showed the opposite finding. And at about the same period of time, "much of consumer research into black advertising has found that whites are not averse to seeing blacks in ads, while African Americans respond more favorably to ads when black actors are present" (Escalas 1994, 305). Research also showed that audiences could detect a whether an unseen speaker in an advertisement was black (Escalas 1994, note 2). Importantly at this point in time the use of Ebonics in ads was looked upon as negative in part because "language attitudes that permeate our society greatly stigmatize vernacular grammatical structures," advertisers did not want to insult target markets and because the decisions were being made about advertising content by non–African Americans (Escalas 1994, 307). Therefore, ads were developed based on white conceptions of what blacks looked and sounded like. By 1999, advertisers had become skilled at interjecting lexical features — i.e., words and phrases without the language structure of Ebonics — into ads. In a study summarized by Williams and Grantham (1999), where the results of research on the impact of Ebonics use in ads was presented, there was a significant interaction between the ethnic identity and race of the advertising viewer who was familiar with Black English.

White America still has a "fascination with" African American expression (Watts and Orbe 2002). By 2002, there had been a tremendous increase in African Americans in advertisements, and these advertisements were not targeted specifically to African Americans. They were actually used to increase a universal appeal that would mitigate differences between ethnic groups and appease Euro American targets in an effort to go beyond color. In an analysis of a popular Budweiser commercial as a constructed spectacle, Watts and Orbe (2002) suggest that the black men in the commercial signify hedonistic consumption through blackness: "That is, references to the ads' 'universal' qualities obscure the way in which blackness can be made to behave in accordance with the American ideology of universalism" (Watts and Orbe 2002, 3), or the new American Dream. Authentic blackness is appropriated, commoditized, and categorically judged as non-important where the dominant can remain *ambivalent* toward it and assuage guilt for racism and social ills (Watts and Orbe 2002, 3) and where dominant people can believe, through a twisted denial process, that they actually identify with the other. At this point in time they believe they are not afraid of black people or ethnic groups taking their place in Green America.

In making blackness a commodity, being black undergoes value escalation only when it can be massively replicated and commercially manufactured (Watts and Orbe 2002, 4). Identity creation comes about right here, when the real need is noticed on one of the positions of Maslow's hierarchy. Blackness and identity are fashioned with safety and security needs, or social needs and egotistical needs, or self-actualization needs. Replication of aspects of blackness to meet a psychological need manifested in consumption serves to associate hip hop dance as a salient cultural cue manipulated onto universal bodies in low involvement product and service branding and appeals. Such connections facilitate all kinds of subconscious pleasures in the form of need fulfillment. The result is that dominant groups are making money and feeling good about themselves and believe that racism is not a problem. Working classes are happy because they can relate to the brothers and sisters in the struggle against capitalism, but at the same time partake of consumption even if they work like dogs. Black people are happy because at least the portrayal is not what it used to be back in the day — or so it seems.

Segmentation (Target Markets) and Impossible Resistance

Target marketing is a phrase that many are familiar with. It is the process whereby people are grouped based on some set of characteristics to be identified as a distinct set of buyers of a product or service. The goal of this type of segmentation is to produce advertisements that will reach the audience, inducing some outcome. Outcomes include, but are not limited to, increasing brand loyalty, brand switching, increasing the amount and frequency of purchase; remaining top of mind or as a part of an overall consideration set, etc. All targeted ads, when developed as a part of a strategic marketing plan, are geared at achieving far-reaching corporate objectives. Methods of targeting and grouping people, of course, can be based on demographic, lifestyle, and ethnicity information, and so forth. People — that is targeted groups — become aware of offerings if they can see themselves in the ad, or if they can identify with the advertising message, source, or some other aspect of the ad that connects the viewer with the utilization of the product or service. Tactics used for these ends include racial similarity, role congruence, intensity of ethnic identification, and shared cultural knowledge (Aaker, Brumbaugh, Grier, 2000, 128). Knowing and manipulating these psychological aspects of consumers, producers of effective ads provide an overall achievement of corporate objectives. Much research is generated on advertising such that the dollars that are spent are not wasted; on the contrary, advertisements used by corporations are not placed anywhere on a hunch or by accident. Using hip hop dance as a means to carry these tactics through the media is no accident either.

However, discussion also arises as to the advertising effects of excluded markets.[11] Feeling excluded from an audience or targeted group has been shown to be detrimental to the purchase of products, particularly when the excluded group identifies itself with the dominant culture. In either case though, the non-target market is likely to feel irritated, ignored, neglected and offended (Aaker, Broumbaugh, Grier 2000, 128). It is not difficult to see that a company bears a large risk in losing that non-target consumer, and in turn not achieving corporate objectives, if the consumer happens to see an ad that is not meant for him or her. The degree of feeling excluded is lower for ethnic minorities. In other words, the dominant group feels excluded more strongly than do minorities when the dominant group watches an ad that has messages and meanings intended for minorities. At the same time, "appeals featuring minority sources tend to lead to more divergent thoughts and less tacit acceptance of the message, which may induce enduring attitude change" (Aaker *et al.* 2000, 129). Ads then that are produced for a majority with the intention of using a minority source, such as hip hop dance done by transracials, can foster consumption in the majority. Such an outcome is much more valued than excluding any group. Additionally, the ethnic market identifies with the sources portrayed in the ad if consumers consider themselves to be a part of an ethnic minority, while people in the non-target market internalize the message if they consider themselves part of the non-ethnic majority. Therefore, advertisers have every impetus to develop ads that reach many groups and exclude none. Given the rapid expansion of hip hop dance around the globe, it is an excellent medium to connect products to, to allow people the feeling of inclusion, and to increase internalization. What this last point means is that the assuaging of the feelings of being excluded is paired with and reinforces a sense of remaining dominant. When the source in cases like this is portrayed as non-ethnic but can do, for example, The Runnin Man, the majority then also identifies with the message. In so doing, the outcome sought by the corporation is more likely to be achieved (Aaker *et al.* 2000, 137).

Not everyone thinks increasing brand loyalty is the goal of advertising, whether targeted or not. The Center for a New American Dream (http://www.newdream.org) suggests that America is trending away from brands and more towards value, value to be had in self identity, and a self identity constructed from resistance. Douglas B. Holt (2002) takes up this topic using a cultural consumption model reiterating voices from Marxist approaches (i.e. Horkheimer and Adorno, Gramsci, and de Certeau), demonstrating the ways in which consumption practices are positioned in our society to keep people controlled.

In reality, the cultural authority tells consumers what to do, rather than consumers telling companies what to produce as part of the marketing concept. Holt quotes a view proposed by Horkheimer and Adorno in 1996, that segmentation is a dominating strategy, and all aspects of marketing seek to erase cultural nuances. Yet simultaneously, everything consumed is part of a code layered onto it by the market. When the goal of advertising is discovered (as in the non-targeted group of consumers mentioned above who got irritated and wanted to walk away from the brand when they realized they were being excluded, duped, or otherwise manipulated) many folks will seek ways to resist the marketing force of the cultural authority (Holt 2002).

Two things come to mind in this reading. First of all, in this economy and society, consumers are always already not liberated from the market. As soon as one believes resistance is possible, the advertising shifts and metamorphoses into yet another message carrying culture. And second, hip hop dance is read by some as being a site of resistance, a sign for it, signifying independence. Indeed "hip hop culture [dance] ... create[d] a 'new vernacular' of 'insurrectionary knowledges' that are juxtaposed to traditional historical societal forces allowing the oppressed to at last 'fight the powers that be'" (Orlando 2003, 402, quoting Potter 1995). This made it a fabulous medium for carrying to the consumer the ideology that personal sovereignty could be had through resistance. Resistance was in vogue and that then became a commodity pushed through a postmodern consumer culture — a culture that valued products that appeared authentic and detached from a paternal corporate machine.[12] Companies suggest, by tying the dance to products, along with all its significations, meanings and messages, that they, consumers, can resist, they are individual selves not caught up in a segmented attempt to push products on them.

In summary, in this chapter the consumption process, the linkage of culture with it, and the construction of identity with the distribution of hip hop dance was covered. The discovery is that we have entered an era of the target market of one, the post-postmodern branding method that seeks to have consumers see themselves as "citizen-artists" (Holt 2002, 81).[13] But this, I would suggest, is a myth and a certain impossibility. Everything bought in the market has a meaning and so, meaning is shifted to include individual resistance and this is marketed on a national, if not global, scale, and commoditized. Corporate objectives are still achieved. Consumers are still buying. Capitalism is still being linked with culture. People can construct any identity, i.e., blackness for a day, if they want to. And the beat goes on. As a rhetorical, let me pose this question again: What identity exactly is up for grabs and for whom?

> Brands that create worlds that strike consumers' imaginations, that inspire and provoke and stimulate, that help them interpret the world that surrounds them, will earn kudos and profits.... Since the market feeds off the constant production of difference, the most creative, unorthodox, singulariz-

ing consumer sovereignty practices are the most productive for the system [Holt 2002, 87, 88].

As has been argued, hip hop dance gives ways to resist, teaches historical methods and theories of resistance, and provides interpretive aspects and meanings connected to social contexts. It facilitates an imagined community. It inspires, challenges, provokes while at the same time supports the capitalist system. Hip hop dance was the perfect cultural lubricant to use to smooth out frictions of labor versus capital, to make consumption of low involvement products smack of hedonism when we work like dogs to increase productivity, and to blur the lines of difference. At the same time, hip hop dance was a great facilitator of the creation of the transracial, a diminisher of the dominant group's fear of being excluded in segmentation, and low lying fruit hanging on a tree they consumed with the knowledge that they remain in control of and perpetuate a system that ensures their supremacy. The dance had power at its inception. Through merging it with consumption of products and services it was not feminized: it was bastardized.

Notes

1. Media means television commercials, product and cultural artifact placements in movies, Internet ads, print ads in magazines, and the distribution of these in the United States and other parts of the world. The portrayal of blackness within these distributions and the theorization of it warrants an entire study. For further reading see Havens 2002.

2. The concept of consumption is multifaceted and must not be taken as given or natural. People consume for a variety of reasons as will be shown throughout this chapter. However, there are metaphors of consumption used in marketing that at the very best lead to only a glimpse of what consumption entails. They include consuming as experience, consuming as integration, consuming as classification, and consuming as play. The experiential aspect emphasizes the felt emotional states that go with consumption of an object (any tangible or intangible purchase can be defined as a consumption object). Consumption integration has to do with the ways in which an object's meanings are brought to the consumption context. It is in this process that one may see tactics occur such as resistance and objectification away from authenticity in the development of a self or social identity (see below). Classification of consumption objects directly points up the ways in which consumed objects classify the consumer relative to how other people they think are important from a social standpoint. And playful consumption facilitates interaction with others under a given contextual arrangement, and can be seen as a performative consumption practice (Holt 1995). These four aspects then will suffice to give a broad brush framework for the idea of consumption.

3. Involvement is a complex aspect of advertising aimed at attitude change. Advertisers want consumers to become involved with their ads because a more involved consumer is

likely to process the information whereas an uninvolved consumer will not. From a practical standpoint, no one can process all ads as high involvement because consumers have filters that allow or disallow information to enter into their psyches. High involvement messages are deemed to provide for cognitive-attitude-behavior processing while low involvement ads are aimed at cognitive-behavior-attitude processing. Cognitive processing occurs through a central route to persuasion; low involvement ads take the peripheral route (Petty *et al.* 1983).

4. Petty *et al.* 1983.

5. Attitudes contain cognitive, affective and behavioral components, or one's beliefs, feelings and behaviors toward an object. Explicit attitudes are those that are expressed and what a consumer consciously believes and will admit to being true; implicit are those that are outside the consumer's awareness (Karpinksi and Hilton 2001). For example, one may state openly a belief in gay marriage, but when given a psychological test for this attitude, implicitly the person's attitude is against it. Advertisers work with all three aspects of attitudes, within both explicit and implicit realms, in promotional messages.

Studies of attitudes enables corporations to predict what a consumer intends to buy. The Theory of Reasoned Action (TORA) provides a way of predicting behavior through the measurement of behavioral intentions toward a consumption object (Ajzen and Fishbein 1980). According to the model behavioral intention consists of two components that stem from measures of attitudes toward an object, and the subjective norms associated with that action. Each of the two components is further divided into two more subcomponents. For the attitude component, beliefs about the consequences of consumption and the evaluation of the importance of the consequences it are measures taken into consideration by the consumer. With regard to subjective norms, or what the consumer believes other people think about his actions surrounding a purchase, normative beliefs and the motivation to comply with them form the basis for its two subcomponents (Fazio *et al.* 1986; Pham *et al.* 2001). Attitudes and behavioral intentions are formed in the consumer by the meanings the consumer establishes for consumption objects. In other words, the consumption means something to each person, says something about the individual personally (Kleine *et al.* 1991, 1993). This can be understood this through a hermeneutic model of established meanings (Thompson 1997), where the cultural frames of reference reside in personal histories and experiences. These in turn lead to the make up of attitudes. One therefore can have multiple attitudes about a consumption practice. The belief component of the attitude measure resides in what people think about a particular behavior.

Once the attitudes towards an object are known, the beliefs about them, and consumers' evaluation of their importance, they can be changed if need be. Attitudes are subject to change (reinforcement) when the attitude object is paired with a more (or less) favorable one through mere exposure (Downing *et al.* 1992). Attitudes can also be changed with persuasion (Friestad and Wright 1994; Meyers-Levy and Malaviya 1999). The key is to know what needs changing.

The subjective norm refers to the person's "perception that most people who are important to him think he should or should not perform the behavior in question" (Ajzen and Fishbein 1980, 57). According to the TORA, when a person perceives that his important significant others think he should perform an act, the stronger will be the intention to do so. Normative beliefs and the motivation to comply with those beliefs influence the strength of a person's intention. It is through the subjective norm component of the behavioral intention that social contexts and self-identity are taken into consideration. Self-identity tends to be reinforced over time in recreated, real, or imagined social situations. It can change over time, although it is usually stable (Ethier and Deaux 1994). Social contexts in relation to the subjective norms provide feedback to the individual engaged in a behavior.

6. Maslow's hierarchy of needs suggests that people have five levels of needs ranging from physiological to self actualization. Theoretically a person moves up the hierarchy only after having filled the lower level need.

7. Berkowitz *et al.* 2003.

8. Kleine *et al.* (1993) discuss social-identity theory at length wherein there is a connection between one's things and oneself. Identity is relatively stable but there are multiple identities that we all possess having to do with social class, ethnicity, sexual preference, race, gender, religion, and so forth that distinguishes us or links us with others (Grier and Deshpande 2001). And importantly, products are functionally related to specific felt identities constructed by people; products purchased gain importance as the constructed felt identity gains importance or salience; and it depends on which identity a consumer is working with at a given time that will manifest and guide the consumer's sense of self. For example, on any given day, a person can simultaneously be a parent, child, employee, president for a non-profit board, etc., which other people read and recognize, and we self-analyze. These identities are hierarchical and underpin three social and cultural (non-natural) states, that is being, having, doing (see J. P. Sartre, *Being and Nothingness: a Phenomenological Essay on Ontology*, 1943, 1956), directly related to the need to consume (Klein *et al.* 1993; Forehand *et al.* 2002; Klein *et al.* 2002). These then are artifacts and props that are used on the dramaturgical quotidian stage, for the contextual role being enacted at any given time, that are affected by who we interact with and the degree to which those interactions affect self esteem. In this reflexive process a social identity is constructed.

9. Consumers often classify consumption practices into necessity, utilitarian, and hedonic needs, or a combination of the three (Okada 2005). Forms of entertainment, such as music, films, television and dance, have the effect of providing appealing pleasurable and sensory experiences for consumers. Including these types of cultural and aesthetic stimuli can increase the effectiveness of ads by linking their hedonic aspects to consumption of what would otherwise be a routine necessity or utilitarian purchase (Holbrook and Schindler 1994).

10. Cues can be source (characters in an ad and for examples their skin color, ability to do hip hop dance, hairstyle, facial structure, stature) and nonsource (items not related to the source at all, such as background, language, music) varieties, and they can be salient or nonsalient. Source cues tend to be more salient than nonsource cues, and they are quickly processed and linked with implicit cultural associations. Of course, depending on the way in which an ad is positioned and other variables, many cues can be associated with the character and become salient.

11. The idea of excluded markets and the problems associated with segmentation practices has been studied by several authors. See G. Cui, and P. Choudhury 2003; Huntington 2005.

12. Commercialization can reduce and eliminate perceptions of authenticity, as in the case of the African art market. Consumer perceptions of authenticity, according to Grayson and Martinec (2004), are of two non-mutually exclusive distinctions and these distinctions are variable at best. Indexical authenticity refers to something not being a copy or a fake, which makes it valuable. Iconic authenticity suggests that something is a replica of an indexical object. And dance in advertising is considered to be iconically authentic if and only if consumers have a prior knowledge schema of how dances from a given culture are supposed to look.

13. Definitions of modern, post modern, and post-postmodern have to do with changes after World War II in the intensity of consumption, economic growth, and colonialism led mainly by the West. This topic will be covered in more detail in the chapter on globalization.

5

Furthering Globalization and Capital Formation

The western discourse on African art denies the instrumental-
ity — material, metaphysical or spiritual — of an African object
once it has reached the western context. In this new setting the art
has no "function" ... African art objects are divorced from their
proper function and original meaning when taken out of context.
African art is no longer valued "instrumentally" or "as a means to
an end" but rather valued for "its own sake" or "as an end in itself."
                          — Christopher B. Steiner, *African Art
                                        in Transit* (1994, 159, 161)

What we have is a paradox in which the anti-capitalist politics of Rastafari [like hip hop dance] are being "articulated" in
the economic interests of capitalism: the music [like hip hop
dance] is lubricating the very system it seeks to condemn; and
yet the music [and the dance] is an expression of an oppositional ... politics.... The politics ... are expressed in a form that
is ultimately of financial benefit to the dominant culture (i.e., as
a commodity which circulates for profit). Therefore ... it is a
force for change which paradoxically stabilizes (at least economically) the very forces of power it seeks to overthrow.
                          — John Storey, *An Introduction to Cultural
                                 Theory & Popular Culture* (1998, 127)

[The] central characteristics of hip-hop's language, musical
traditions, oral culture, and political location make it a black
American form. In fact, the history of white artists is a history
of their speaking to the black Americans....
                          — Mickey Hess, *Hip-hop Realness and
                                  the White Performer* (2005, 375)

130

Skin, after all, is the basis for discrimination. Color has haunted Americans since America's inception. I recently heard on National Public Radio a newscast that reported on a case being brought before the Equal Employment Opportunity Commission about a darker-skinned African American who filed a discrimination suit against a lighter-skinned African American at an Applebee's restaurant near Atlanta, Georgia. The lawyer at the EEOC was saying that there had never been a case brought only the basis of color. Then they had other experts, you know how they do on NPR, saying that it would be difficult to prove that type of discrimination because you had to show that the person accused of discrimination recognized that the person being discriminated against was of a different complexion and that it was the basis of maltreatment. I think it is peculiar that no case has been tried before the EEOC on the basis of skin color. Even more, it is fascinating that the so-called first case of color discrimination is between two African Americans.

Announcing: Daisy Does America—*A new show on TBS that you won't want to miss! This week Daisy goes hip hop with the brothers.*

Scenes of Daisy, a European, blond, long haired, young woman with an English-Scottish-Australian accent traveling through America getting the entire experience—the black inner city experience this week.

She is outfitted in large diamond jewelry necklaces with pendants that reminisce upon—signify—gangster rappers and pimps. She is given the 411 about how to make moves, hip hop stances, hip hop dances, rapping, sporting corn rows and sweat suits.

No female, but only male images projected, black men with cockeyed baseball caps, gold teeth, and "the black man's walk," hanging out on the city streets with nothing to do but show Daisy how to do America.

Whites with all the money are not in clubs dancing. African Americans and other African-Diasporaed people—at least some of them—are. But you have to look long and hard to find a club with African-Diasporaed people unless you are in the inner city. It is not hard to find hip hop music and dance in the suburbs or in international tourist dance clubs with absolutely no black people in them. Pasadena, Riverside, Temecula, Moreno Valley, Mira Mesa, Lee's Summit, Stuttgart, Joplin, Cancun, Montreal, Rotterdam only make up a short list of where you can consume hip hop dance and music in a club with no black people in it. Okay maybe there are two or three black people up in there. That is nothing compared to the 500 in there altogether. So if African Americans, who created hip hop dance and music, are not in these clubs then who is?

Well let me tell you who is not in those clubs. No this is not a longitudinal cross sectional study of hip hop dance clubs but rather a report on what I have observed and observation is a valid consumer behavior method; you can look at the bibliography if you want references. I would do a longitudinal cross sectional study if I had the money or if I had grant resources for it. Alas I live in reality and I am not dreaming. Anyway, go ahead. Look around in these clubs like I did in LA, Montreal, Pasadena, Cancun, Rotterdam, Riverside, Kansas City. You have your Mexicans, Asians, Middle Easterners, and then you have your working class whites — in other words, "The Post-Modern Others" all acting like blacks. Or trying. They are not like those trying to be black for a day because they are hated too. You have women in there half dressed, men in there with baggy clothes, always a black man on the wheels of steel. Some time you got two or three rooms of different music being played. Like one room with disco, another room got top 40 and another room got hip hop. The hip hop room is the most crowded with women writhing around trying to move like images of black women, DJ telling you to throw yo hands in the air and party like you jus don't care, mixing that in with whoop there it is, and dancing men trying to be cool like a black man.

It used to be that being black was not what anyone wanted. And I aver that it is still that way, only some want to play make believe that it is not. Then it became cool to be black, or at least to be able to talk, dress, and dance black. But only if the actual artifacts that point to these African American activities can be bought for personal use and put away when not convenient. And it used to be that blacks were the lowest group in the world. Now it seems that, through the process of commoditization of bodies, on an economic level, many people are like blacks the world over. It used to be that folks with non-black bodies, within the United States and outside of it, who suffered from economic disadvantage, wanted the American Dream of success, a house, a business or job, a place to raise their families in religious peace. That was the capitalist carrot dangled before the working classes so the rich could beat them harder with sticks. That, as has been shown, is still the case but now it is dressed in a different costume: the costume of identity construction with resistance using the African American cultural artifact of hip hop dance. Therefore here I demonstrate the process of cultivation of African American artifacts for sale and concomitantly show how this informs the new American Dream of colorlessness, African slavery in absentia, sustained with mental colonialism and consumerism.

Background

African Art in Transit, written by Christopher B. Steiner in 1994, is an ethnographic study of the physical production, distribution and sale of African artifacts from the West Coast of Africa to Europe and the United States. The text and research set forth in his book points out the market relationship between buyers and sellers, the value of making an artifact look as if it had use, and cultivation of the value of that use for economic gain. Such a market is a constructed one, with sellers having more knowledge about the products than the buyer, but one in Steiner's assessment that positions the African trader as "a cultural mediator between two groups brought in contact through common economic pursuits" (Steiner 1994, 155). The goal of the two groups is to exchange something of value. The market segments that purchase African art place value on the artifacts to the extent and degree that the object can be read as indexically authentic; that is, that the object has been *used* in African life and not merely manufactured for sale so that Africans can accumulate capital.[1] It seems that the reason purchasers seek assurances of authenticity is so that they may distinguish between the value of art intrinsically and the value of art as an investment in satisfying the need to consume and minimize risk. Simultaneously there is a separation between the functionality of the art object as it was intended and a psychological distancing of the buyers from indicating that they want only indexically authentic objects, what would be called consumption with cultural disassociation (Watts and Orbe

2002). The result of this complex interplay is what Steiner defines as commodity fetishism, the worship of commodities. Moreover, this commodity fetishism psychosis is found in the development of self-identities where one group can buy pieces and parts of another group while leaving aside unfavorable social and historical events. Commodity fetishism aptly describes what happens to African American objects of art and African American ways of being when placed into the system of capitalism and separated from their contexts. Purchasers of African art adorn their homes, galleries and museums with creations of African peoples. Similarly, purchasers of African American art buy ways of being, speaking, and moving; they adorn their bodies in the West, and many other parts of the world, with these objects; and they create ways of being separate and apart from the context in which African American art is or was created.

Furthermore, like the process described by Steiner within the constructed African art market, there are multiple market dynamics taking place in what African Americans produce for use and what they produce for sale. The problem lies in being able to capitalize on the distinction between the two activities, a problem that *Cote d'Ivoire* Africans have clearly figured out. Here I want to address several bodily and artistic ways of being that have a use for African Americans but when they enter into the capital formation process are stripped from their use and become ends in themselves. These include skin color, plastic surgery for bigger buttocks, breasts, penises and lips, hairstyles, language, and hip hop dance: the phenomenon of being able to buy aspects of blackness like one buys a pair of socks, black for a day, moment, or other temporary period of time.

Moreover, stereotypical and schematic characteristics associated with being black for a day are also sold through films. For example, *Save the Last Dance* where the white girl wins a coveted position with a top-notch US ballet company — by incorporating into her audition watered-down hip hop dance moves taught to her by her African American boyfriend. Or the movie *Hitch*, where the white guy wins the rich woman in part because he is able to execute hip hop dance moves. These kinds of movies along with media statements presented in the last chapter about hip hop dance erase the meanings of the texts as they were originally written. Even so, they are entrenched, embedded, imbued in the very culture of America.

Application of these ways of being and artistic achievements onto bodies outside an African American context allows for the purchasers to be black for a day without understanding, caring or concerning themselves with what it is like to be black for a lifetime, let alone to be able to comprehend centuries of mental and physical racial challenges. But before that, to understand the commoditization of African American artifacts — specifically hip hop dance — two major concepts explained by Karl Marx must be employed and engaged, in an abridged format of course, in the dialog. And, to understand the commoditization of bodies, a brief review of the process of slavery must be taken up. Both inform this chapter.

In his work *Capital* (1977), Marx critiques aspects of capitalism that are a result of commoditization which can be applied to the black for a day phenomenon.[2] Marx describes the differences in the creation of commodities and the creation of money. Depending on what part of the transaction comes first, you are either producing something for your personal use, use value, or producing something to increase your capital, surplus value. The former begins with a purpose generating use value — like doing b-boyin or b-girlin in the street to rap music. This is writing about a variety of social concerns, and not seeking to increase capital accumulation but seeking something else, perhaps embodiment of historical recordings. Or the creation of a piece of fabric to use in daily life. On the other hand, the latter, producing something to increase your capital, begins with a purchase and ends with a sale, like buying raw materials to make the fabric to then turn around and sell it for a profit. The purpose is the creation of exchange and surplus values, the aims of the capitalist. Please note by the way that not all capitalists are white, nor are they all male.

It is this type of transaction that motivates the capitalist to peddle African American wares for profit, impels him to attach African American movement to the sale of commodities, and definitely entices him into selling records and videos featuring Gangsta Rap and hootchie mamas to audiences comprised of youngsters. These same Marxist principles can be applied to many other ways of being, other African American artifacts, aside from dance and performing arts, such as jazz, blues, theater, etc. The point is to keep these concepts in mind as the chapter moves through those African American artistic forms and ways of being.

Via consumption practices people can use their money to enjoy aspects of blackness like hip hop dance without incurring the social consequences of actually being black, while at the same time, increasing surplus and accumulation. Much of this consumption is tied, as mentioned, to social identity that is calculatedly placed, and finds its way into media messages designed to reinforce or change mass levels of demand for goods and services. Advertisers want to reasonably predict what is going to be purchased, how much, by whom and when.[3]

The use versus surplus value dichotomy knows no bounds. Human commoditization is defined as the transformation of a human being into the property of, or under the control of, another person or institution in order to extract accumulation and surplus. Aspects of a human being taken under the control of the commoditizer include the person's freewill, self, body, skills, abilities, and in extreme cases, reproduction. The process itself assumes that the commoditized body enters the cycle first as an autonomous being, with the ability to make choices and decisions freely. Then through a series of mechanisms either friendly or not, the body becomes initiated into a depersonalized status and then given a new identity. At the final step, commoditization of bodies is reinforced over time forcing maintenance of the individual's mental, emotional, and physical acceptance of himself as commodity. At this point there can be oppositional forces, wherein some commoditized bodies resist, some resign, and some vacillate between these two options. It is clear however that only a certain amount of resistance will be tolerated by the commoditizer (Hirschman and Hill 1999).[4] And the whole underlying reason for commoditization is the accumulation of surplus.

In any event, the steps of the commoditization process, and its ultimate aim of increased profitability, can be achieved in part by manipulating consumers' behaviors through consumption. The black body has been commoditized and this of course is not news. Now though a large contingent of laborers are being commoditized as well, overseas, in Mexico, Third World areas, China, and Western white people are being commoditized. All are waking up and seeing that they too are used for surplus value creation, and the whole racial construction is nothing but a con. They have no money and no power. Black body parts, hip hop dance, and African American culture are being used as the cover. The next section problematizes the use of black body parts and culture, their commoditization and their consumption.

Skin, Hair and Language

"None o' y'all [white people] will trade places with me and *I'm rich!*" says Chris Rock in that same 1999 comedy performance referred to in another chapter. Some interesting studies that we could think about in terms of how people distance themselves from actually being black would be the following. Study with hypothesis one: If the surgeon general wanted everybody to stop smoking or doing bodily habits that are defined as detrimental, all he would have to say is if you continue, your skin will turn black. Everybody and his mother, those who are not black, would stop those habits in a heartbeat. Study with hypothesis two: This would work with all people, not just Euro Americans.[5]

However, there are literally thousands of non-black and non-brown bodies that go to tanning salons on a regular basis because they want to have some color — be almost but not quite black. It is a multibillion dollar industry (probably not a service industry dominated by African American ownership) where people lie in a tanning bed that is giving off man-made ultraviolet light rays that mimic sun rays and temporarily change skin color: a darkening of the skin. The industry is composed of not only of tanning bed manufacturers, but also those that manufacture lotions so one can apply them to one's body in an attempt to control the degree of blackness one acquires, as well as to hopefully ward off or limit the skin cancer diseases associated with overexposure to harmful rays of light.

II. Hip Hop Appropriation

Skin is a protective organ of the body that has differing degrees of pigment, which dictates its color. The amount of pigment one body exhibits is defined by what that body's DNA requires. DNA is not discriminatory but people are. Take skin off bodies and they are indistinguishable on the basis of color. Africans living in the region of the world they live in, as well as other people of color, developed levels of pigment and DNA coding that would protect their bodies from harmful rays of sunlight. That is all skin color is. But Euro Americans have continued to find ways to capitalize on it and use it to contribute to surplus values and separations. Remember also that a whole industry of commodities exists for black people trying to be less black. Creams promising to lighten the skin, peels promising to do the same. The fact that some African Americans have bought this ideology and therefore use color of skin to value or devalue someone else, even those of their own family and community, speaks to the insidious nature of hegemonic discrimination on the basis of color. It is like anyone's mother used to say when a complaint came out about not being able to do some of the things other children were doing: "Well if they jumped off the top of a skyscraper would you want to do it too? And the other children don't live here; now go on in the front room and do what I told you to." Just because some Euro Americans place value on light skin does not mean we must follow suit. It is important that we keep in the forefront of our minds that skin — an organ of the body that has a function and use just like other vital organs of the body — is a major basis for commoditizing bodies and developing market segments. Can you imagine someone saying, "Well, you are inferior because your pancreas is darker than mine"?

If skin is bad, hair is worse. Like skin, we need hair to protect parts of the body and again the place of one's origin on the planet dictated to one's DNA the type of hair needed to cope with the physical environment being lived in. Besides the use of African and African American hair that it provides to the body, artists have created hair designs to both facilitate the quotidian task of African American hair management and to exorcize us from the false notion that straight hair is better. These artistic endeavors have now crossed over to allow Euro

138

Americans the experience of being black for a day without the lived experience of being discriminated against for having bad hair. Artistic African American hair designs such as corn rows, weaves, and extensions enable African American women, and in some cases African American men, to function more easily and acceptably in a society that values straight, long blond hair. But it is not unusual to now see women who have DNA coded straight hair to fashionably select corn rows or extensions and styles that speak of African American hair art. But you do not see these women in corporate America. Rather they are seen on vacation or some such activity. Many African Americans have adopted the dreadlock, which is a Jamaican artistic form of hair management. It has become more and more common for European descendents to wear these locks. Does placement of artistic African-descendent hairstyles on to European-descendent people speak of any use value for them in wearing the style? No, it is a form of bodily commodity fetishism.

Commodity fetishism of African American art and bodily practices is not limited to essential body parts or appendages. Ebonics in terms of how it relates to enslavement and signifying practices has already been discussed. I also mentioned that often people, African American people who speak Ebonics, are considered dumb or stupid or both if they speak this language. But when non–African Americans speak Ebonics, they are considered to be on the cutting edge of popular culture, able to communicate on an artistic level that separates and distinguishes rhetoric from reality. People outside the African American culture seem to resort to speaking bits and phrases of Ebonics when they really want to get another person's or another group's attention, when they want to be hip, cool, or appear to possess the ability to converse on a level un-definable through standard Euro American English. Ebonics has a certain use value among its native speakers. This use value has been manipulated into surplus value in thousands of electronic and print media and political campaigns, allowing the black for a day phenomenon to continue to have currency without consequence. Since this circulation of Ebonics is a reality, we should recognize its beauty as a language, perhaps even interpret it as an African American artistic form. Certainly the poetry of rap lyrics consisting exclusively of Ebonics, and being bought by mainly European descendents, is a main source of international circulation of the language. Hair, skin and language then are aspects of blackness being made into products for consumers. These body parts have nothing to do with surplus value creation but they have been twisted into the process, with abject disregard and dislike for the body from which the extractions occurred.

Hip Hop Dance

In the next chapter examples of hip hop dance and the codification process will be covered in detail. Here for now, note that this process is doing just what has been done to African art, skin color, Ebonics, hair and other African or African American art forms: hip hop dance performing art is absorbed through capitalistic commodity bodily fetishisms and is therefore disassociated with the creative and artistic energy that was used to develop it. These artistic forms which have use value for users are separated as Steiner defined (1998) and for reasons that Jane Desmond makes clear in her edited 1997 volume *Meaning in Motion.* Capitalistic commodity bodily fetishisms allow "middle and upper class whites to move in what are deemed slightly risqué ways, to perform, in a sense, a measure of 'blackness' without paying the social penalty for being black" (Desmond 1997, 37). Such fetishism also underwrites the dominant culture's need to remain supreme, and mitigates their fears of being excluded in segmentations. At the same time, skin color plays the major role in discrimination by sight. Denial of the use of Ebonics language plays the major role in discrimination in education. Images of beauty limit financial success for both men and women. Hair type limits the ease of African American movement into economic America; an advertisement in *Ebony Magazine* (August 2001), which Johnson Products would not give permission to reprint here, depicts an African-descendant woman with straight hair and poses the question of whether she got her job because of her resume or because of her "relaxer."

The cultural artifacts have value, but experiences of people who create them do not. Yet and still Euro American purchasers want assurances, as in the African art trade, that what they are getting is authentic. Is the person teaching the hip hop dance class black? They want to know. They may as well be asking if the commodity they are paying for is authentic African American performing art; however they are not asking this question because they are concerned with reading and understanding hip hop dance text. It rarely stops them from paying for the commodity if the instructor is not African American. The consumers of hip hop dance lessons value the performing art separately from the context in which it was developed, and separately from the experiences which developed it. Learning hip hop dance in a sanitized suburban dance studio is void of use in the Marxian sense, just as African art sitting on a shelf is void of use.

And forget not the baggy clothes phenomenon that swept the world as a result of jailed African American men who wear loose fitting coveralls represented by rappers on street corners. Now, the required attire for hip hop dance lessons are color coordinated baggy clothes. While glancing across many a space, from college campuses to communion services, one sees baggy fashions. Ask any person how the baggy clothes fashion came to be and you will probably get some kind of dumb look from them. Another example, somewhat different but still to the point, is what Anna Scott writes in "Dance," her 2001 contribution to *Culture Works,* about Euro Americans' addiction to owning black beanie babies, porcelain mammies and metal coon clocks which are called "African American Collectibles nowadays" (Scott 2001, 123). Hip hop dance and the clothes that go with it are of that caliber now.

The protagonist in Spike Lee's film *Bamboozled* (New Line Home Video, 2000) sums up why certain people seek black for a day experiences: "Black people set the trends in the US." These trends in music, dance, fashion, hairstyles and so on are profitable for the myriad of suppliers capable of capitalizing on the trends and turning them in to accumulated surplus value. This is also why resistance means nothing in the long run. And as already argued, African American hip hop dance forms have shaped the social dance scene globally, and influenced both

American concert and social dance genres. Brenda Dixon Gottschild's work attests to this (1996, 2005) while writer and scholar Robert Farris Thompson calculates that "12.2 percent of our population, black Americans, are consistently responsible for more than 50 percent of our popular music" (Thompson 1996, 213) and Geneva Smitherman estimates that whites buy 71 percent of all rap music (Smitherman 2000). These statistics are significant, deep, and profound, and should be critically evaluated against the statistics facing African Americans which consistently and historically situate African Americans coming up short economically when compared to whites.[6]

It is of no value to get into a discourse over the fact that with trends being set by us, still we have many African Americans — talented trend-setters — living in poverty and despair. What deserves emphasis, again, is the notion that some people can buy these experiences — rap music, dance, hairstyles, language and fashion — without being required to experience being black. How would it feel to you to be able to, if you are African American, to be able to wash off the black, decide what clothes you want to wear or get your hair cut in such a way that you do not have to worry about whether your hair, that is your natural hair, is going to keep you from getting a job, "go back" if you have a straightened do, or drip if you have chemical additives? As that *Ebony Magazine* advertisement for a hair straightening product implied, though some African Americans are being employed with artistic hairstyles, if a woman shows up to an interview with hair the employer cannot understand, her chances of securing a job significantly diminish. A sad commentary, aside from the statement the advertisement makes, is that the advertisement appeared in a publication that has historically been known as an African American pillar of journalism, a magazine that is supposed to be down for the peeps. Being black for a day, an hour or a minute is very different from actually being African American. Peddling African American bodily practices is now an end in itself.

Separating hip hop dance from its context strips the African American culture of a valuable resource, namely a way of writing and documenting history. True, hip hop dance has been and is being commoditized and sold. But that does not negate the fact that since

Africans were dispersed from Africa, dance has been a source of language and communication. It helps to keep the processual approach to this in mind: what has the change over time been with respect to African American dance? Besides making more money for certain privileged folks, and expanding the global acceptance of African American social dance, not much. What I mean by that is that hip hop dances are texts that *still* speak about something going on in the African Diaspora experience since the African Diaspora can never be revoked nor people compensated for it. The difference is that now the African-Diasporaed are situated within advanced capitalism and globalization. What this means is that capitalists do not understand that they are teaching the history associated with hip hop dance with its very production portrayed in the media. In other words, African Americans have succeeded tactically in globalizing a way of teaching African American history.

Sites of being black for a moment through dance and African American movement show up in really strange places. Consider commercials for products such as iPod, DM2 (digital music mixer), Sprite soft drinks, McDonald's, MP3s, Kodak cameras, and Pepsi. Just recently I saw a billboard advertising a healthcare company where the white male doctor was slapping a high-five with a white male child. What slapping a high-five has said and taught since its choreographic inception (which was developed by African American men) is that "You are right" or "I agree with what you are saying" or "Great job!" This movement text affirmed the participants and came about at a time in the late 1960s and early 1970s when the only affirmation to be had was from each other. Now we see the use of the text in ways that allows being black for the moment as a way to affirm a purchase and even select a doctor and to reduce cognitive dissonance.

Signs, Signifiers, Difference, and Deference

Globalization and formation of capital via hip hop dance is completed by the signs, signifiers, and differences between people portrayed in circulated media representations depicting African Americans and

Euro Americans. Three world-renowned French theorists who have done extensive analysis on the use of words in language can help make a point in this regard. Ferdinand de Saussure divided language into two parts: the signifier and the signified. The signifier is the word and signified is the image we conjure up when we hear the word. Hip hop dance can be labeled as a signifier, and what is signified are sex, drugs, violence, and white girl rape by black men (see the movie *Traffic,* Universal Studios 2000). Words (signifiers) plus the images (signified) we conjure up constitute what he called the sign. For example:

- Word=Hip hop dance (black people).
- Image=black people engaged in sex, drugs, violence, and so on.
- Sign=danger, poverty, loose women, uneducated, non-white, bad.

These relationships between words, images and signs are arbitrary, established by "cultural agreement" amongst the privileged and the underprivileged. Even though these types of signifiers, signified and signs exist in American culture, trying on hip hop dances and African American derived cultural practices in the privacy of one's home or in a suburban dance studio can be done without risk of erasing constructed differences; it allows for social identity formation or reformation and cultural agreements while simultaneously yielding capital accumulation for the seller of the dance commodity. What has been historically accepted about black people is shunned by people with incommensurate experiences based on imagery from signs, while at the same time takes on new meaning when veiled by capitalists' desires for profit gains and when watered down for consumption.

However Roland Barthes believed that signifier, signified and sign produce connotations. As such, signs can signify multiple meanings depending on who is reading them. So consider then that if one dances hip hop dance, and if one is not of African descent, it could connote not a break with the accepted Westernized patterns of power, but rather it can connote being cool, like when white men are shown doing The Cabbage Patch in a television advertisement for Internet services. This becomes linked with the social identity and the new American Dream.

Jacques Derrida (the "always already" theorist) sees the sign as both deferring and differing. Meaning is always deferred, never fully present, giving intertextual transference of meaning. As such he believes signifiers and signs are meaningful only when read in a discourse. Discourse halts the continuous deferment of signifier to another signifier: you need binary oppositions to understand meaning. As for example in Gangsta hip hop dance music videos with hip hop dance in them, the so called bad guys moving in the video in reality are the whites but they are characterized by the African American men. Meanings over capitalism are redefined in such a way as to depict African American behavior as resistive and violent and solidify Euro American behavior as supremely correct through the discourse of commercial hip hop dance. In these videos, one can use a gat, steal, and kill cops to get over by any means necessary, while at the same time enjoy the hedonistic consumption promised when the meanings are transferred to consumption, and without any risk of being black. *They are signifyin about the capitalists.* An *emic* hip hop dance reading can be interpreted as signifiers and signs writing and reinforcing difference, placing a mirror before the power structure to redirect the gaze as a resistive strategy, and at the same time deferring to the meaning and history of being African American. But these movements are meaningful only when read in the discourse of historical texts and without it the *etic* texts circulate. Hip hop dance circumvents needing binary oppositions because it is a teaching text that always already encompasses the experiences of African Americans, even if those who perform it are consumers being black for a day.

Labor and Commoditization

In any event, the production of signs, signifiers and signifieds for mass production and dissemination, as any other capital-generating commodity, needs labor and hip hop dance is labor intensive. Picking up again and continuing with Marx's analysis, he says labor power is the use of the human body to manufacture use value of any kind, whether for capitalistic gain or not. If the body is being used to create surplus value, then it is seen as a commodity. If the body is used to create personal use value, such as when hip hop dancing is writing history, it is not a commodity. On the other hand when the body is used in production, it becomes labor. Labor is a commodity like corn, which is owned by the individual but is grown usually to be sold in the market place. When separated from the context of use value then, I assert that rappers and hip hop choreographers are commodities used to produce profits. Capitalists selling products "sponsor" programs and "front money" for videos and commercials of "all skin tones, making dance steps into stepping stones of market-share success" (Scott 2001, 112). The capitalist does not care why a laborer presents his labor for sale. The capitalist does not care about the content of rap songs or the texts of the dances, only the resulting profit. The only properties of the artistic forms she cares about are that those total inputs used in creating her product are considerably less than the surplus value gained. Unlike the capitalist, labor — hip hop dancers and nobody knows me rappers — typically possesses no means of production like recording studios, television studios, record labels, land, machinery or capital. It could be possible that African Americans' lack of ownership of other salable commodities and their related and necessary distribution networks contributed to the rise of globalization and commoditization of hip hop dance though I cannot state that emphatically. Nevertheless, historically rappers and hip hoppers did not own any means of production and often they produced records and videos without due compensation and without control. However, some do now own certain means of production for the creation, distribution and sale of hip hop culture, and they are perpetuating the accumulation framework. Like Biggie Smalls would have put it, there ain't no beef with that. But overall, the means of production still rests within the hands of Euro American men, a fact that clearly jumps out of the data showing the number of businesses owned and who owns them in the tables presented in the previous chapter.

Because rap music vinyl and compact discs are easier to mass produce and yield larger surplus capital, and it is logocentric, hip hop dance became separated from the rap music. But commoditization of hip hop dance is in effect. The capitalist has found ways to accumulate it several ways. Immediate examples include sales of instructional videos and dance lessons in white owned studios offering hip hop classes. Purchasing these commodities allows hip hop dance text to be appropriated and provides black for a day experiences in the privacy of the home, or within the safe, ain't-no-black-people-here space of the studio. This is not to say that all hip hop dance lessons are offered in the suburbs or in Euro American studios. They are not. What I am saying is that learning commoditized hip hop dance in a studio affords the art form the beginnings of new connotations in the consciousnesses of Euro Americans and forces it further away from gaining acknowledgement that the dance, when written by historically enslaved colored bodies on ghetto street corners, in African American house parties and at African American social dance clubs, serves a use and provides historical teachings.

Products are essential outputs of labor under a capitalist framework and as said earlier, they must yield a certain level of surplus value in order for their production to make sense to the capitalist. Moreover, whatever labor produces belongs to the capitalist to whom labor was sold. (Sounds like slavery, does it not? Or should it be called commoditization?) Since rap and hip hop dance have moved into the commercial world, much like African art has moved into the commercial art trade, the product of rappers is vinyl or compact discs. Many rappers know when they are producing something strictly for sale in the commercial market and make the conscious decision to do so. They also know and consciously decide when they are producing something for use and those are the poetics that typically are called underground rap and have deep social commentaries written in Ebonics. This behavior is not very different from those *Cote d'Ivoire* Africans who produce African art strictly for sale. They know what they are doing and go to great lengths to make the artifact *appear* as if it were authentic. This is the way that they have used the capitalist game to their own ends. Rappers do a similar thing.

What products do the labor of hip hop choreographers and dancers produce? Aside from the product of studio lessons — a child who can successfully do The Runnin Man, for example — products of hip hop choreographers and dancers can be seen in sitcoms, films, dance videos, commercials, rap music concerts — media representations — and in hip hop-only staged performing art. In media representations, hip hop dance functions in the background being seen voyeuristically and thereby adding surplus value to the commodity represented in the media. Hip hop dance acts as a lever to raise the value of what we have seen in a commercial, promoting purchases of computers, soft drinks, hamburgers, or enrollment in a healthcare plan. Use value of hip hop dance is separated from its created surplus value by negating or minimizing the notion that hip hop dance teaches history and it is useful as a text for passing history along among African and Euro Americans alike. When separated from these historical texts, power remains with the dominant and therefore ensures mitigation of opportunities for upward movement by millions of African American laborers into higher levels of the American social strata. Hip hop dance gathers surplus value as it moves from the African American community into the global economy via media representations. Even so, some African American hip hop dancers and choreographers make the conscious choice to sell their labor to the capitalist knowing that they have to give the illusion of producing authentic dance while knowing that they are not, just as the Africans do in *Cote d'Ivoire* where there are whole warehouses, kept out of view, full of mass produced artifacts that are sold as authentic treasures so that the black for a day or collectibles in commodity fetish can be carried out to support the construction of identity.

Appearing in proscenium-staged hip hop dance performing art, hip hop dance viewing is paid for by consumers but these consumers are paying for use value rather than surplus value because it is not mass produced and subjected to accumulation of surplus value that takes place in global production and distribution of media representations. Often times, in addition to choreography that means something through the artistic talent of the choreographer, choreographed hip hop dance concerts give tributes to the history of African Americans and the audience values the performing art as a text in and of itself, and begins to have the effect of allowing hip hop dance to be seen as an art on par with dance arts such as ballet. Hip hop dances of the early period, say between the 1970s and 1980s, are reconstructed much the same way as a ballet that was choreographed in the 1900s is reconstructed. Having said that though, hip hop dance staged within a proscenium is quite different from the intent of hip hop dance developed in urban streets speaking and teaching history of economic oppression. More about this difference is the basis of the next chapter.

Multiculturalism

If the capitalist's goals are to reap profits by whatever means necessary, then it is necessary for them to solidify their labor force in the manner of what Marx calls co-operation. Using hip hop dance is a way that can facilitate the solidification of the global multicultural labor force and strip the meanings away from the dance movements themselves. While African Americans have known for hundreds of years the impact of capitalism on one's life means that you will work for a good portion of your life without as much as a thank you, that the American Dream of owning the means of production is a weak promise and lofty goal, other newcomers to America and laborers around the globe who are now being swallowed up by the labor portion of the profit equation manifested through capitalist expansion seeking greater and greater surplus value, may believe it will one day own it. I remind my friends who think they are middle and upper class, regardless of their ethnicity, that they are at best three months from being homeless if they lose their jobs. Promising labor that they will one day be rewarded, while at the same time tricking labor into thinking it needs to consume, is the greatest lie perpetuated next to the notion that there are differences in people due to their skin color or genital endowment. True, there are a few African American owners of businesses, such as record companies, media companies, manufacturing companies and the like. But, as the statistics of African American business presented in the previous chapter show in the most recent year for which data is available, we own businesses that produce only 4 percent of all sales in the United States. By and large we are laborers in and out of the United States, own nothing in substantial quantities that will allow the time to homelessness to be reduced or the balance of power to shift from Euro Americans to African Americans to women or any other group. So the capitalist, without saying anything about where and why it was developed or what it says of economics, gives us hip hop dance videos and rap music commercially produced and globally distributed to promote co-operation among those of us that "have not" for real, and those of us that "have not" but think we got it going on.

With the spread of global capitalism more people around the world both been exposed to the myth of ownership and wealth, and capitalism has arrived on their doorstep. For example, Africans in *Cote d'Ivoire* are engaging in African art trading with the Western world using the capitalist model, and as a result some of those African art traders are able to own houses, cars, and clothes; many more remain less fortunate, i.e., Chinese, Indian, Russian, American, etc. Generally though, capitalism expands its reach to incorporate more and more workers while at the same time acculturating them into aspiring to be capitalists while simultaneously holding them down with consumption requirements. After being slapped into the realization that the myth of wealth does not exist for them, perhaps by having to labor but not having enough food to eat, or having lost a job (or the ability to provide subsistence as in certain agricultural societies) due to technological improvements or other efficiencies in production, many more people around the globe know that they will never own the means of production and never be wealthy. And if you cannot be wealthy then you should at least look wealthy and look like you own the means of production. The taught and learned desire — it is not a natural desire — for material goods is not new. The taught and learned desire to consume goods is well documented in Sidney W. Mintz's 1985 ethnographic study of sugar consumption. He documents in that work the growth of the global sugar industry where enslaved labor was used to harvest sugar (who were forbidden to consume it), and the ability of paid labor to consume sugar was a signal to labor that they could be like wealthy Europeans. Before long though, the ability to consume sugar by paid and enslaved labor became so important that people up and down the social ladder needed to consume sugar in order for the capitalist to be assured of his profit. I interpret the consumption of sugar at the time as a kind of glue that held enslaved and paid labor together in order to allow for more consumption of and therefore more production of sugar and therefore more profit. Owning and consuming sugar was a way of feeling like you had arrived but also made labor efforts somewhat more palatable if you could have sugar before work, during work and after work. If production of sugar was halted then the outcry for it would have been so great that the masses would have turned on the capitalists in outright revolt. Interestingly, we do not even think about sugar production today or what it means to consume or not consume it. Today, sugar does not hold global laborers who produce products for profit together, nor does it attach itself to other products to increase their production as it once did. Instead, the ability for laborers to consume hip hop culture and the ability for capitalists to attach hip hop dance and music to their products does.

The hip hop dances that are being used to opiate the global labor force concurrently divulge the history of capital accumulation that has taken place for years. It just so happens that the art form materialized through African Americans. From a multicultural point of view, as more people get a glimpse of the empty promise of capitalism, which African Americans know full well, more resistance to the capitalist comes about, which in turn creates more pressure on the capitalist to keep control of the workers. Capitalists use hip hop dance as a way to keep control of the workers through pushing a multicultural agenda. We can all get along as long as you keep working and turning out profit. It in no way matters what your skin color or genital endowment is. Hip hop dance has been usurped by a psychological strategy of the dominant, allowing labor to let off steam to ensure the continued sale of and production of his products, which by the way includes those in use for being black for a day, and the maintenance of the global human commoditization process.

Marx has pointed out that workers' labor becomes a commodity, a specialization of the process of production takes place, which creates the division of labor. This division of labor resembles the division of classes in society, and serves to reinforce and solidify the classes found in the society. More is produced in less time, and a collective, mindless worker emerges. Tellingly he writes in *Capital:* "The man whose whole life is spent in performing a few simple operations ... generally becomes as stupid and ignorant as it is possible for a human creature to become. [The work] corrupts the courage of his mind ... the activities of his body.... This is the state into which the labouring poor, that is the great body of the people, must necessarily fall" (Marx 1977, 483). What better way to distract labor from the stupor into which it falls than by pushing a multicultural agenda, lubricated with hip hop dance, set up on the false precept that people of all cultures are important? The truth as I see it is that the multicultural agenda pushing global labor to produce and consume, supported by hip hop dance and music, is simply an agenda toward more exploitation of labor in the name of capitalistic global expansion and the denunciation of the creators of African American performing art.

bell hooks speaks of hopelessness, a yearning, pervading many people's lives, especially those who are oppressed, but certainly those who once were oppressed and now are seemingly not, who feel powerless to change the racist ideologies that exist, that create divisions of class within and amongst African Americans and by extension it is assumed that this includes oppressed classes around the globe. How do we solve the problem of fragmentation amongst people in this society which oppresses people but denies it? A good deal of this fragmentation comes from the taking of African American creativity and making it into commodities. "That many other groups now share with the black folks a sense of deep alienation, despair, uncertainty, loss of a sense of grounding ... cross boundaries of class, gender, race" (hooks 1998, 420) could be a means for solidarity, hooks suggests. That is a valid and agreeable conclusion. And it is because of these overwhelming feelings and facts that hip hop dance has had such a strong global impact in unifying a real community of oppressed and marginalized people.

Essentially Modern or Post-Modern?

Would the craze for hip hop dance be called modern or postmodern?

Is being black for a day or a period related to postmodernism? It could be if we look at it as change from seeing black as signifying danger, something to be shunned socially, to something connoting value. Just what is modernism and post-modernism? They seem to be terms which have no definition but at the same time have multiple definitions. The definition for post-modern that I can grasp the easiest is the one that seeks to equate the movement of capitalism to underdeveloped, undeveloped, primitive and exotic, or war-ravaged lands, where the International Monetary Fund has been or lurks just behind the next release of a particular nation's failing financial figures. After the successful delivery of capitalism to these spaces and geographic locations, then they are post-modern. They have been subdued into the capitalist fray. But there are more definitions of modern and post-modern. The writers of these definitions seem to be talking to a closed audience, like rap singers who make rap songs that speak specifically to a particular MC or OG. The purchasers of the songs are just the audience, innocent bystanders who like the beat, or who witness a drive-by shooting. And like rap music, unless you are part of the lived experience of gangs and socio-economic lack, you cannot understand what the rappers say to each other in closed but packaged conversations on CDs. Your experience is incommensurate.

To give an example of ways modern and post-modern definitions slip we can evaluate African American movement texts. The Black Power Fist was modern but was misread and labeled too militant and was shut down by the dominant power structure. Here you have a movement choreography of an arm extended above the head with the hand balled into a fist. This movement spoke of the history of powerlessness and the desire to give power to the people. Everyone who raised their fists in this manner wrote that history. To African Americans then, modern was to be able to write the dance and have it be read nationally and internationally. Post-modern came with the shutting down of the modern; no more fists but yet we had "peace" with two fingers. There we go, African Americans oppressed again in new and creative ways and ridiculed. So, "[I]t has become necessary to find new avenues to transmit the messages of black liberation struggle, new ways to talk about racism and other politics of domination" (hooks 1998, 419). Some people think that the medium for this new way of talking about The Struggle is available only to African Americans via African American music. On the contrary; there are other ways of "talking." Like through writing both inside and outside academia, speaking and writing in Ebonics, and writing and speaking through hip hop dance. All of these approaches must be engaged if we are to survive, and if we are to affect the canon with post-modern theory the oppressed can relate to through our lived experience. Hip hop dance is an unrecognized theorization practice that achieves this.

While on this topic of post-modernism, we may as well revisit essentialism. "Essential — the fundamental nature of something; a theory which stresses indispensable conceptual characteristics and relations of things as opposed to existence as particular experienced actuality" (Webster 1991). Let us be mindful that the black experience is not post-modern and certainly is not essential, since all African Americans have different experiences, and there are marginalized people all over the planet. It is because of these different experiences that we have today, coupled with the one experience of the African Diaspora and the one experience of the US Black Power movement, that makes for diverse cultural productions, and avoids broad categorizations of African Americans into neat little boxes of signifieds. This is what is post-modern. Note that this positioning of post-modern theory is non-binary and necessarily eliminates marginalization. Not fitting in neat little boxes of homogenous blackness assures the sale of artifacts, i.e., hip hop dance cum commodity, have less surplus value generation capability. And moreover, it reduces the human commoditization process as a whole, along with separate body parts and ways of being.

Racism and discrimination have existed for a long time in many parts of the globe. That is not news to no body. What used to happen in, say, Egypt in terms of slavery was limited to the immediate eyesight of the inhabitants under dominance. With the increase in capitalistic ways of production, that is with increased efficiency and more surplus value creation, the first media technologies were developed, and through them information was more rapidly disseminated. Books and newspapers were once considered the cutting edge of technology. But with the creation of mass produced books and newspapers, according to Benedict Anderson, we have the beginnings of imagined communities. As theorized by Anderson, global capitalism has created communities of impoverished post-post-modern people who find value and meaning in their lives by identifying with hip hop dance texts. The technology has facilitated this identification true enough, and Anderson was asserting that the community was imagined because many of the people within these similar communities would never meet each other face to face, never hold a personal conversation. Be that as it may, there is nothing to be imagined about the effects of capitalism on poor working classes. Transnational corporations have learned that they move their capital to the physical location on the globe that yields the highest return on their investment. If that means transracial people in Mexico design your car, people in Argentina put parts of your car together while people in Indonesia manufacture the fabric and FedEx ships it to the US, then so be it. Or if it means that transracial women in Taiwan can assemble computers for Microsoft while they grow their hair for sale in support of black for a day hairstyles, so be it. If African art is in demand then the global market will find a way to meet that demand. If people in India are forced to buy post-post-modern genetically engineered seeds to plant subsistence crops and forbidden to plant anything else to their detriment, so be it. If the Polish people have to pick asparagus that the Germans will not pick but they will eat, so be it. And if adapting hip hop dance pushed through media becomes a way to appease people and indoctrinate them in Western consumption practices in the imagined and real communities of poverty, while simultaneously being sold as cultural artifact allowing for black for a day experiences, for entertainment, so be it. The transnational corporation or multinational corporation is interested in one thing: ensuring its own survival and profitability. As such, global capitalism has brought to many what African Americans have experienced for centuries. In these regards it could be said that the world needs hip hop dance as text.

At this post-post-modern plateau, black people have done something great. They have written history, theorized, strategized with their bodies until it could be done with their oral communications. And just as African Americans gave us a way to protest against social ills when the Civil Rights Movement began, African Americans have given people where capitalism hits a *parole* and *langue* to express meaning, a way to deal. Moreover, African Americans have created a vehicle to generate and collect the unstoppable quest for profit. Their body parts, ways of being, and hip hop danced texts, are now used in identity creation, colorlessness denial of the ongoing practice of human commoditization, and rat race consumption in support of a new global American Dream.

Notes

1. The topic of indexical authenticity has been covered in the preceding chapter.
2. Several definitions will help. These definitions are paraphrased:

- Commodity — something (person or thing) that contains a specific quantity of objectified labor which is exchanged for a quantity of money equivalent to wages (costs) to the commodity itself on the one hand, and profit to the capitalist on the other (Marx 1972, 954).
- Use-value — something that one derives utility from, and cannot be separated from the commodity (Marx 1972, 125).
- Surplus-value — relative and absolute — is the value over and above the use-value (subsistence earnings) of a commodity, that which can be directed to the bottom-line profitability of an enterprise. Relative surplus-value can be derived by becoming more efficient in production while absolute surplus-value is produced by lengthening the production run and workday without increasing wages (Marx 1972, 437).
- Capitalist accumulation — converting surplus-value into capital (Marx 1972, 725).
- Primitive accumulation — the origins of capitalist accumulation; the initial accumulation that allows one to become capitalistically accumulative (Marx 1972, 714).
- Means of production — the instruments of capital (money, labor, machinery) required for the creation of goods, services, arts, and dance (Marx 1972, 981).

3. The Theory of Reasoned Action (Ajzen and Fishbein 1980) covers the predictive nature of consumption. Please see notes in the prior chapter for a full discussion.

4. This is precisely why resistance as a strategy is only able to give the capitalist more ways to control. As has already been explained, all marketers do is capitalize on resistance and a new cycle begins.

5. As a matter of fact, my dear uncle will not drink coffee to this day because he was told when he was a youngster that coffee will make you black. Aside from this anecdotal trivia, there are research studies that measure people's implicit racial beliefs and find that many people, including black people, do not want to be black. See Karpinksi and Hilton 2001.

6. See the earlier discussions for demographic statistics on African Americans.

6

Hip Hop Dance Codification and Commoditization

Even when there is no sustained or professional training in dance technique, dancing is still coded, stylized and appropriated in social and cultural contexts.
— Janet Wolff, *Resident Alien: Feminist Cultural Criticism* (1995, 82)

Continuing along this line of thinking about hip hop dance, Sally Banes said in *Writing Dancing in the Age of Postmodernism* (1994) that the global circulation of hip hop dance was distorted and fragmented. She further suggested that when read correctly and with commensurate knowledge it gives us a view of history of black dance encompassing the shores on the parallel sides of the Middle Passage areas. Banes spoke in the context of break dancing mainly, but the same can be said for much of hip hop dance. She further suggested that as of 1984, the dance could be learned by videotaped lessons. Suburban women and professionals were also taking hip hop dance at the YMCA or studio. These facilitated a hip hop dance losing its currency and value in terms of a read and interpretable text. The way you could tell that hip hop "gained a foothold in mainstream America" was that it appeared in dance studios (Banes 1994). Searching for ways to distinguish hip hop dance before and after media attention homogenized it, and in essence commoditized it, Banes coined the terms "prefame" and "postfame"

(1994, 138).[1] Prefame, as she describes and has been alluded to here, is the dance text that writes history. Postfame hip hop dance is what we see on TV and in certain types of movies and music videos, in neighborhood dance recitals, and in instruction videos such that "theatricalized and sanitized, it emphasizes gymnastics over meaning" (138) such that "popular moves become standard" (156). Additionally, validation of "the spread" of hip hop dance is seen in studies such as *Une Ecole de Danse Hip Hop en Banlieue* (1999) which is a report about hip hop dance in the suburbs of France. Also, Valerie Orlando (2003) researched the use of hip hop dance and culture in the Banlieue cinema. There is also a study entitled *Berlin Goes Wild* (1998) which discusses hip hop dance in Berlin, Germany. These and other documents about hip hop dance capture, on one level, the lengths that hip hop dance has traveled over the Earth and indicate that its travels are nowhere near finished.

What is evaluated in this last chapter is the codification of hip hop dance, that is, the systematic arrangement of rules of teaching, dancing, and displaying it, and the making of it into an article of commerce. Examples of how live hip hop dance is staged in dance recitals, concerts, and in education are analyzed. To evaluate and review these aspects of hip hop dance, information and findings from an interview with Rennie Harris, artistic director of the hip hop concert dance company PureMovement in Philadelphia, Pennsylvania, as well as an interview with Ben Reid, Jr., a hip hop dance studio choreographer with Bre Dance Studio in Riverside, California, will be drawn from. The experiential findings that I had with teaching hip hop dance in an elementary school will be given. Observational findings of hip hop dance class methods in suburban dance studios will be presented. No analysis of codification would be complete without discussion of hip hop dance instruction videos, therefore this will be addressed as well. In contrast to studio, video, concert, and educational environments for codification of hip hop dance, some talk about hip hop dance in clubs will be set forth. Hip hop dance and the process of codification and commoditization will be briefly compared to ballet instruction and consumption, making the argument that instruction is meant to train bodies into replicating African American bodies that produced hip hop dance, as in a similar fashion ballet sought to train bodies into replicating royalty. And finally a glimpse of how the funding of the codification of hip hop dance took place, as compared to that for ballet in the United States will be presented.

Studio and Video Instruction

Earlier chapters presented in this book have documented that hip hop dance was conceived on the curbs, corners, and passageways of inner city streets. This would be the last thing thought of if the Yellow Pages were opened to the heading of "Dance Instruction." A large percentage of the commercial dance studios found under this type of heading, whether they are in fitness centers or public parks, teach some form of hip hop dance. For example, in the city of Riverside, California, which is a suburb 60 miles east of Los Angeles, there are some 25 dance instruction facilities and at least 20 of them offer hip hop dance or funky dance. These may be classified as jazz dance if the owners of the studios do not want to be too risky in positioning their businesses.[2] In the city of Temecula, situated halfway between Riverside and San Diego, there are comparable numbers of commercial facilities offering hip hop dance instruction. In Moreno Valley, a city immediately adjacent to Riverside, a commercial dance facility is located in the Moreno Valley Mall (with anchor retail conglomerates such as Sears, Robinsons May, along with other standard mall shops such as The Limited, Casual Corner, etc.), and it offers hip hop dance. I have personally observed five such suburban studios in southern California —*Bre Dance Studio* in Riverside, *Backstreet Performing Arts* in Riverside, *Temecula Dance Company* (located in a gym comparable to commercial fitness centers where I did not see even one African American) in Temecula, *Kathy's Dance in Temecula*, and *Ballet Theater School of Dance* in Moreno Valley. Each of these commercial studios offers some form of hip hop dance instruction six out of seven days per week. There are classes designed for particular age groups, as in youth hip hop, adult hip hop, teen hip hop, team hip hop, and instruction comes in beginning, intermediate and advanced levels. In several cases, as with the *Temecula Dance Company*, their hip hop dance classes out numbered all other studio instruction courses in frequency, number, and duration.

Of the five studios I researched, only one of them was owned and operated by African Americans: *Bre Dance Studio*, where the hip hop dance classes were taught by African American men and women with the majority of the students being African American teenaged boys and girls in equal proportions. All the other studios held classes taught by Euro Americans and were owned by Euro Americans. In all cases, classes include children and adults, five years old to forty-something arranged by age and ability. Generally speaking, the Euro studio class participants were Euro American girls and women. What I also witnessed was that the use of music, on more occasions than not in non–African American studios, was not African American hip hop music — Gangsta or commercial — but something else. Instead it could be compared to aerobics music used in teaching low-impact: the kind of music that has a strong repetitive but non-complex beat designed specifically for exercise.

In codification, a costume emerges. As for students of hip hop dance in Euro American studios, they wore athletic clothing or loose-fitting street clothing like shorts and tank tops, along with sneakers or athletic shoes or work boots. This outfitting was designed to reflect clothing worn during hip hop dance sessions that were impromptu, meaning, those done on inner city streets. (As importantly, the line of clothing itself became commercialized and commoditized, as evidenced by the number of people wearing hip hop style.) Codification further includes the attempt at constructing a hip hop body that signifies black bodies. Those bodies are strong, lean, and muscular but not overly so. They are rhythmic and able to execute syncopation. The ability to hold one's weight upon the arms, as in walking on the hands or doing pull-ups is highly valued. The hip hop body ranges from about five-feet-five to six-feet in height. Women tend to have small breasts and small behinds.

These hip hop dance bodies in formation in the Euro American studios stood about arms' length from each other on the studio floor.

The more shy dancers stand in the back and the ones who feel more confident stand in the front. The class began with a warm up. Shoulder rolls, grapevines, stretches and other types of moves seen in aerobics classes constituted a portion of the warm up. They used jumping jacks or skipping around the studio several times to get their heart rates up. After a sufficient warmup, the instructor began creating a series of movement combinations that resulted in a choreographed set of body designs that did not look like prefame hip hop dance. That would be expected since they were choreographing postfame hip hop dance. Watching closely, one could see remnants of The Snake, The Cabbage Patch, The Roger Rabbit, The Box Step, The Bounce, The Pop Lock, The Robot, some b-boyin and b-girlin and so on. But one would have to watch very closely or one would miss them.

Transitioned from the warm up, the participants attempted to mimic what the instructor did. This would be reflective of the creative process discussed in the chapter theorizing hip hop dance, and could be a primary, secondary, or tertiary degree representation of the dance within a historical or non-historical context. The codification process followed in this case would place it at the far end of either of these spectrums, i.e., tertiary reproduction and non-historical contexts relative to African American writings in a postfame and *etic* framework.

In one studio observation, I witnessed the instructor trying to teach the five- to seven-year-old, middle class Euro American girls how to call and respond, using "hey, ho" phrases. She was also trying to teach them how to "add a little funk" to their moves while one of the mothers looked in on the class from the hallway and smiled approvingly. The instructor, blond, blue-eyed and tanned Miss Kym, taught the girls to move into their "C" which resembled the African and African American cipher where dancers encircle dancers who come into the center of the cipher and write texts. She did not reference any African American contexts, and the "C" lasted only for a fleeting 4-counts as the girls traveled into another formation of staggered lines of dancers. There was no emphasis on the torso or hips. They were getting ready for a recital they were doing in the newly built theater funded by and standing on the property of the Catholic Church; at that recital 20 percent of the program was hip hop dance (sorry, no photography allowed during the show but the video will be available for sale in the lobby for $25; that is why there are not any pictures of it here), mixed in with ballet, tap, and jazz. In preparing the little girls for their "Picture Pose" to be taken before the actual recital, Miss Kym had most of the girls stand in a hip hop dance freeze, arms crossed and legs slightly apart, all body weight on the left leg and foot. Those girls who were not standing squatted down with their hands on their knees. She encouraged all of them to show "some attitude" and made them practice several times so they would "remember what do to when asked to get in their Picture Pose." As in ballet, the body must be aligned properly and the head must move just so, for instance. For example in ballet, the back is straight, the hips, buttocks, and abdomen are tucked in. The neck is elongated and the shoulders back but pressed down. Arms are held as if toothpicks are in the armpits. Legs are turned out from the hips and the weight is placed on the balls of the feet. Theatricality is also emphasized for instance, the way the dancer is to gaze, and where to gaze. Improper preparation of the body and lack of theatricality will result in improper execution and delivery of the choreography. Body technics and theatrics are just as critical to the correct execution of hip hop dance. However, for a number of reasons that could be problematized, such a systematic approach to teaching and choreographing in the studios covered here, at least, did not exist. Therefore, what instructors said in their attempt to develop a hip hop dance body technic and theatricality were phrases like "get low" or "show some attitude" without uttering the signification "like black people do."

In Euro American hip hop dance instruction, great emphasis is placed on being able to count. Each instructor first demonstrated what each body part was to do on each count. Students of all ages were drilled several times with counting and moving their bodies. Once convinced that the participants knew the counts, the instructor turned on the non-rap music. In the case of the five-year-old girls, they were taught to count out loud and coordinate those counts with their bodies. When the music was added, one of the girls' mothers was sitting on the periphery of the dance studio mouthing the counts for the girls. In contrast, on the other hand, counting was not the emphasis at *Bre Dance Studio*. Ben Reid, Jr., started out moving with rap music playing and expected his students to follow his choreography and timing. They did. This is how many hip hop dances are learned in many African American homes, clubs and at house parties; that is, by watching and reading someone else.

The mirror dominated studio focal points, as it does in ballet class. Dancers were looking at themselves in the mirror while they danced. Since their focus was on themselves they were concerned with perfecting their moves, and following but modifying the instructor's choreography, not theorizing their own texts. This directly relates to Foster's (1998) description about choreographic intent, skill and the impact that dancers have on creation of something a bit different than what the choreographer wanted yet still containing the choreographic signature. We should easily realize that there were no glass mirrors in the writings of African Americans theorizing hip hop dance on street corners, at house parties, or other locations where the dance was being written. There were other intangible mirrors however. The dance was reflected back to the dancers in terms of correctness and execution. At the same time it served as a reflection of what was happening and had happened to African Americans in America. And finally but not inconsequentially it served as a mirror for Euro America.

And some folk want to be able to do the moves and not see themselves in the studio mirror or even let their other friends know they doing them. That reminds me of a time when I was taking pictures of some hip hop dancers at *Bre Dance Studio*. There were some middle-aged white women — who had brought their daughters to learn hip hop dance — in the hall just outside the studio practicing some moves together in secret. They would not let me take their picture and giggled and blushed at my inquiry.

Now, if one is not comfortable taking a hip hop dance class, then it is really simple to learn hip hop dance through the medium of instruction videos. There are many of them that you can find on-line and in stores that sell physical fitness instruction video tapes. The first thing I noticed about some hip hop dance instruction videos is that the names of the instructors were weird. I mean, they are meant to sound like they are, in my opinion, African American hip hop dance instructors, you know, cool and all that.

You can, for example and depending on your needs, buy funky, urban or simply funk hip hop, aerobic hip hop, strictly choreographed hip hop, kids hip hop, hip hop that you learn so you will not be embarrassed at a club, groovy hip hop in three volumes, street style hip hop in two volumes, hip hop grind, tai-funk aerobics hip hop, freestyle hip hop, three hip hop habit dance videos, and my personal favorite, *Yoga Booty Ballet*. In that last one, the white female middle-class looking instructor promises, in front of a backdrop of other white female middle-class looking students, to let you really express the *real* you. Of course this is not an exhaustive list.

Generally the instructors on hip hop dance videos are not those African American people you see in the inner city whose bodies give accounts, where you hear helicopters and sirens, witness drug deals, hear gunshots and cars passing by with rap music so loud you can hear it two blocks away. There are exceptions of course, and one of them comes to us from Fatima's hip hop dance instruction video and I will get to her in a minute. Generally speaking though, hip hop dance instruction videos follow a similar pattern seen in Euro American studio taught hip hop dance classes. Matter of fact, there are videos for sale that teach instructors how to teach hip hop dance, and teach judges of newly arriving hip hop dance competitions how to judge. It is no wonder that hip hop classes look like videos! Anyway, videos often start out by telling you that you should warm up, and advise you to check with your doctor before beginning any exercise routine. The instructor promises to show dynamite hip hop moves slowly, from the front and side so that you can learn quickly, and then do them at tempo. If you get discouraged, just rewind the tape, they say. When they get going, past the counts and the way they match the movements, they put on the music. Often, I do not recognize the music as rap music, either underground or mainstream.

Usually several other people (generally not ethnic) are standing behind the typically Euro American instructor, and they all have on loose-fitting color coordinated clothing. The men sometimes have hats or do-rags on their heads; the women have tank-tops or navel revealing tops on. Their postures try to replicate hip hop dance postures evidencing cool, don't-give-a-damn attitudes. The instructor tries to help the learner think "hip hop" by using words like "get low," "think sly," "be smooth," "old school." Coded hip hop dance vocabulary uses either verbally or bodily, thriller moves, Pop, The Box Step, The Cabbage Patch, and The Robot. In addition to these coded African American but not mentioned as such movements, ballet words such as *pas de bouree* show up: evidence the codification process and the gradual affiliation of hip hop dance outside the social sphere of African America and into the theatrical. Again as in the studio, counting out the movements is the primary way to learn how to put the dance on one's body. I recognize that counting is a pedagogical tool for teaching dance of many genres but my emphasis on it here is to exaggerate the difference between pre- and postfame hip hop dance. People standing on street corners, at parties or in clubs are not sitting around counting out the moves before they do them, let alone counting out the moves without music.

The space of this book does not allow me to examine in detail all the hip hop dance videos or all the hip hop studios. I will, however, analyze and criticize one. Fatima Robinson's video *Go Fatima* gives viewers the opportunity to learn portions of choreography used in popular Aaliyah and Backstreet Boys hip hop videos. *Go Fatima* features more African American and people of color dancers, equal numbers of males and females with hip hop bodies. The attire varies somewhat. In some cases, the dancers are all dressed in the same attire with signals for men and women coming only from headgear. In other cases, the differentiation comes with women's abdomens showing. In another clip, the dancers are doing hip hop dance in clothing that looks like Renaissance wear. Women wear long full dresses with corseted bodices while the men wear britches and long-sleeved ruffled shirts which are open to expose their (muscular) chests.

Fatima does not begin with a warm-up, does not begin her first routine with counting, and gives no warning about checking with your doctor. She demonstrates the movement and then puts the music on. The dancers are staggered so that there is no geographic shape represented. She does not tell you how to acquire an attitude or to get low or funky. She relies on her expertise with choreographing hip hop dance videos for Aaliyah, the Backstreet Boys and other popular presentations that demonstrate her "authenticity" as a choreographer. Interestingly though, parts of the choreography remind me of ballet. In the Aaliyah piece, there is a *pas de deux* and a *pas de quatre*, complete with lifting. There is a section with what looks like the *corps de ballet*, a section for the women support dancers, a section for men and a section of the dance for Aaliyah, who serves as the *prima ballerina,* so to speak. It is remarkably similar to the patterns seen in theatrical ballet but uses hip hop dance movement vocabulary, hip hop music and gendered clothing from centuries ago.

The demand for hip hop dance instruction is tremendous. This is not only evidenced by the number of dance studios that supply hip hop dance classes and the number of videos available on the subject. Online one can find chat rooms, bulletin boards and hyperlinks where people from all over the world are inquiring about where they can go to learn hip hop dance and connecting to them with one click of the mouse. Hip hop dance on the Internet allows one to visit sites where hip hop dance instruction can be learned around the globe, and where a dictionary of codified moves can be downloaded for break dancing. And if that is not enough, MrHappyFeets gives you e-hiphop dance instruction along with a study guide complete with a workbook, a video and an audio guide. These materials are available for beginning, intermediate and advanced levels. Of course you must pay for these by subscribing, and cyber MrHappyFeets promises that lack of rhythm will never be an issue for those who utilize his electronic form of learning hip hop dance.

The presentation of hip hop dance in buildings, on the World Wide Web, and on videotapes suggests to me that the codification process has begun. Further, presentation of hip hop dance in these ways significantly waters down the message of hip hop dance written on inner city streets, making it palatable for those who wish to be black for a day to swallow. And again as Brenda Dixon Gottschild (1996) points out, there comes a point when looking at a dancer, for example the lead female dancer in *Save the Last Dance* (2001), becomes an exercise of digging for Africanist presences and the mixture of Africanist presences with European (or other nationalities) becomes a statement of being "all up in each other's other." Some hip hop dance instruction makes me think it never came from where it did and never said what it said.

Nevertheless, a hip hop dance instructor teaches aspects of African American history regardless of how watered down it becomes, or how much Ebonics written in hip hop dance texts becomes translated into English hip hop dance text. For example, when Miss Kym had the little girls move into a "C," that was African and African American history. When dancers in class or on video perform hip hop texts like The Pop Lock, The Bounce, The Snake, The Runnin Man, The Box Step or The Cabbage Patch, they are teaching masses of people African American history via bodily statements from African American tacticians, commentators on signifying about Euro Americans, and lessons in coping with life after diaspora. Other moves are codified and I consider them punctuation in the dialog and commentary. For example, The Arms-Crossed-Over-The-Chest with "an attitude" is one of the potent periods in a hip hop dance text. Standing with feet much wider than the width of one's shoulders Bent-Over-with-the-Hands-on-Knees is a comma. Throw-Yo-Hands-Up is a semi-colon, and The-Step-Hop-Jump-from-Side-to-Side a definite question mark.

Interestingly, hip hop dance codification does not include much ado about the hips. I have not found one instruction segment that teaches The Dog or any variation thereon. Infrequently, like in *Yoga Booty Ballet*, you see some torso contractions being attempted, but they look like a different text. It seems that arms, legs and shoulders are fair game, but instructors generally avoid getting the torso and pelvis involved. In the rare instances that the pelvis is engaged, it is moved from side to side rather that forwards and backwards. Torso contractions similarly remain, when seen, with the mid-abdominal section or focus only on the shoulders. The Sea Walk and The Crip Walk remain curiously absent from the commercial studio vocabulary. You may remember that I theorized these two dances as writing, respectively, about the Middle Passage, and economic oppression. Abdominal and pelvic movements, the Middle Passage and economic oppression speak stereotypically too loudly about being African American, so it has been said, and tells too much truth. Or it could be simply that they are too difficult to do. In any event, they are avoided texts in suburban hip hop dance studios, instruction videos and Internet cyber classes.

Hip Hop Dance — Elementary School Experience

Thirty sixth-graders who had never done hip hop dance were eagerly awaiting me when I arrived at a local elementary school. The grant program sponsored by the university approved my proposal to teach hip hop dance as text and economics in conjunction with African American history to these elementary school children. After I got over my initial shock of a positive response, my next feeling was terror. I knew that there would be no African Americans in the class, and suspected that the teacher was Euro American. I was really thinking that maybe, because there was a demand for it, this teaching hip hop dance as text in conjunction with some African American history, maybe the teacher was African American. I was wrong, of course. But it was a perfect set up because one of the measures of success the administrators of the grant program used to assess its instructors was through a pre- and post-vocabulary test taken by the students. The content of the vocabulary list was totally up to the instructor, but has to be at least 30 words long (I asked if we could use movement vocabulary; but no). Students were given an exam over their knowledge of the vocabulary on the first day and the same test was repeated at the conclusion of the term. This was great. Of course I chose words such as slavery, capitalism, unemployment, cabbage, ghetto, rhythm, patch, do-rag, bounce, emancipation, social, lyrics, history, Ebonics, beat, etc. I will not bore you with the whole list, and suffice it to say that most of the children did not know the definitions of these words at the outset of the program.

The term lasted about 12 weeks and we met once a week for about two hours each week. During the course of our weekly meetings, I invited Rickerby Hinds, creator of the hip hop opera *Keep Headz Ringin* to come and speak to the children. He taught them about African ciphers, beat-boxing, sampling, and making do with what you have to come up with texts and art forms. Without question, I invited a male hip hop dancer to come and teach some b-boy moves and to help the youngsters feel the music, and explain that certain messages were embedded in the lyrics. I had done most of the work teaching them the text and meanings of The Box Step, The Runnin Man, The Bounce, The Cabbage Patch and The Snake. The hip hop dancer I invited followed that up with explaining the messages of The Crip Walk.

The dancers were really excited about learning not only the texts of the dances but also African American history associated with the dance. I showed them the Rodney King video tape, some documentaries about hip hop dance and helped them to understand what happened with OJ. All of what they learned was performed at a school assembly. The performance included verbal and written texts with Ja-Rule's *Living It Up* (2001) as the accompanying music.

We warmed up to rap music, some of which the boys, there were about 16 boys and 14 girls, brought to me. And immediately after warmup, I moved right into showing them the texts with the music playing but I was doing it in a kind of slow-motion. They caught on. Then after a few tries (like about 10) I would bring the text up to tempo. No counting was done whatsoever at this point. Instead we had lessons on the difference between beat and rhythm and they practiced bobbing their heads, clapping and tapping their feet simultaneously while isolating one shoulder then the other when some rap music was playing. And I had to teach them what to think, like think about an aggravating or frustrating experience over which they had no power to change in order to get them to replicate the accent of the text. It is difficult to teach another body to speak a different language.[3]

By the day of the performance they were coming close. At the performance the dance historians that were performing (the students) were excited. They knew the dance sequence, some history and theory of

Africa, African Diaspora, and African American experiences. They knew something more about economics and language and dancing with some socially contextual knowledge. Parents, friends, and other family members were invited to the assembly. Classes were brought in from grades four through six. All of the school's dignitaries were there. On that day many of the parents expressed to me that they were so glad that I was teaching their children how to speak through dance. More than one parent confided in me that "this hip hop dance class" had changed their child's life from negative to positive.

Hip Hop Dance History in Concert

Several dance historians were in Philadelphia in the summer of 2002 for a Society of Dance History Scholars conference. I do not know if it was planned by the conference organizers to take advantage of it or not, but it just so happened that Rennie Harris was conducting his annual hip hop dance conference at the same time. I went to the SDHS conference because I knew I would be able to see "Illadelph Legends: Honoring the Source," which Mr. Harris stages every year during his conference. In his opening remarks he gives the audience, primarily Caucasian but with other ethnicities clearly represented, a definition of hip hop: knowledgeable is hip, and dance is hop. Hip hop can be read as "knowledgeable-dance." He then informs the audience that there will be an intermission, but that there is no formal set-up to the performance; much of it will be improvised. He says though that even though it looks unorganized, there is an organization to it.

The performance is meant to bring to the proscenium the history of how hip hop dance unfolded during block parties and on street corners or other public spaces. Therefore lots of people are milling around on the stage and people are sitting on metal bleachers that are supposed to be stoops one would sit on to watch hip hop dance in the neighborhood block party; a DJ is on stage scratching and making the break in the music last as long as possible so that new music was created and while people wrote their texts. Most of the dancers were African American; some were Latino and some were Asian or another ethnicity that was hard for me to read. It seemed like there were more men than women, but not by a large proportion. The point of the performance was for Harris to showcase and historicize African American men who have been credited with authorship of certain hip hop dances, and cover the history of hip hop dance texts from their inception on the street to about 1980. These texts included The Pop Lock, The Robot, and Crazy Legs to name a few. Importantly, b-boy and b-girl moves were prevalent.

During intermission the stage remained full of people, again replicating inner city life, writing to DJ-ed music, and two of the dancers brought their children up to the stage. The children, one boy and one girl, could not have been more than three or four years old. With encouragement, the little girl executed a move where she held her body parallel to the stage floor using only her right arm; the little boy busted b-boy moves that only a 24- to 36-inch person could. It was incredible to see the virtuosity of these children and their precocious (as compared to those who learn hip hop dance in a Euro-studio or from a video) understanding of the language that writes hip hop dance as texts. Clearly they had been learning the language already for a good portion of their short lives. I am sure they could not count yet.

Harris was kind enough to agree to talk with me over the telephone not long after that concert. I asked him questions about what his company does. He shared with me that he had been doing hip hop since he was a pre-teen and kind of fell into *PureMovement* in response to his own experience with life as an African American youth; the company does not have a school and does not give classes, does not have a plan about how the company will go and he prefers to flow with it. *PureMovement* tours 10 months out of the year; most performances are dependent on who showed up and rehearsal is limited. Harris wants to avoid commercializing hip hop dance. "Commercial hip hop is not authentic hip hop," he remarked. I think Harris brings hip hop dance as text to the stage in a form that is totally postmodern and tactical, if you will indulge me those words. He is not concerned with making the performance look Western, other than using the Western presentation format, but wants to keep it outside the system as I talked about in a prior chapter. Moving it to the proscenium loses some of the nuances hip hop dance as text has in the neighborhood, club or social setting, but it also brings hip hop dance into equality with other theater dance performing art, such as ballet.

Hip Hop Dance Packaged Commodity

Expansion of hip hop dance into studios supports its continued codification and in order to do that it needs funding. I want to take a leap and make a spin here to examine the commoditization of hip hop dance and explore the ways in which it is similar to the commoditization of ballet. First of all, keep in mind that while wealthy people of the European Renaissance were having grand dinner parties and balls where the most elite people performed and observed ballet, Africans were "dancing" on slave ships, on plantations, in dance halls where African and African American women were being "courted" as concubines for European and Euro American men to the exclusion of African American men. Today you do not see people doing ballet at a wedding or a party — but you used to. Today you do see people doing hip hop dance at real and filmed weddings and parties (see the movie *Hitch* 2005 for example), but hip hop dance is also seen on stages, in the background of media (see the advertisement for Vonage Internet cellular service, for example, where a white man in the background is doing hip hop dance), in the foreground of commercials as has been discussed, and as the subject of books.

Dancing masters were the conduits for ballet instruction and the technique was transported rather slowly as compared with today's standards. Some dancing masters wrote manuals to describe the ways in which the dance was to be done, and some manuals exist today, and the men who wrote them have been credited with documenting the codified movements. Over time, with the use of the manuals and personal experience, schools of ballet were established to teach people not only the movement of ballet, but the character or attitude needed to perform ballet well. Bodies were defined by height, weight, foot type, flexibility and so on. Certain movements were designed to create a body that exemplified the message of ballet, like the straight back and stilled hips, with the weight placed over the balls of the feet. And ballet was at one point dominated by men; this changed as time progressed and in the United States and many other countries, ballet is seen as a woman's dance. As ballet began to take on an international acceptance, moving from Italy to France to Russia to Germany to Great Britain to Australia and to the United States it began to become more commercialized and commoditized. Before the commercialization and commoditization, however, the costs of ballet lessons and performances were borne by the royal class; the king or queen of a particular empire paid for everything. The language of ballet has been codified in the French language for centuries so that if one takes a ballet class in any country, the movements are called by their original French names, for example, *demi-plié, pas de bourrée, glissade,* etc. As the economic model began to shift from the crown to capitalism, people who enjoyed ballet were increasingly faced with having to buy a ticket for consumption of performances or pay fees for consumption of instruction.

Ballet companies from other countries had toured in the United States in the early 1900s; however, it arrived in the United States in the 1930s and 1940s, but not by slave ship. Because ballet production was expensive and ticket sales did not cover all of the associated costs, foundations were soon established by wealthy individuals that supported the expense of producing and learning ballet — Ford, Rockefeller, Mellon, Chase, and so on — which provided sponsorships to select ballet companies so that they could teach children ballet technique and stage performances in well appointed theaters.[4] Contributions to ballet companies by the wealthy classes in America were seen as philanthropic and were beneficial as tax deductions for the contributors. And even though current contributors additionally seek some sort of recognition for their contribution they understand that a ballet production is usually a not-for-profit situation.

During the 1960s, the federal government created the National Endowment for the Arts (an offshoot in recollection of the defunct Federal Theater Project of the 1930s which allowed many African Americans the opportunity to stage their performing art) that funded many a dance company in their pursuit of dance training and staging.[5] Keep in mind that in the 1960s great upheavals were taking place against racism and many Americans were dying from their conviction that the way coloreds were being treated was wrong. John F. Kennedy, Malcolm X, and Martin Luther King, Jr., were assassinated during a high time of legislated funding for staging ballet. African American dance was taking place in venues very different from ballet presented in theaters. True, the National Endowment for the Arts provided funding for a few African American dancers and all-black dance companies who were able to perform in theater venues. But this number was proportionately smaller than the funding going to individuals and companies offering ballet performance and training. Some of the money that was funneled into ballet was to allow the teaching of ballet to youngsters. Do not forget that the Ford Foundation was established around the same time, and it was a great supplier of funds for ballet training and performance.[6]

Legislated delivery and instruction of hip hop dance, however, is not the name of the game as it was for ballet. Nevertheless, many of hip hop's dance steps are codified in music videos and movies, young people learn the codes in studios, and it is now presented in prosceniumed theaters. Hip hop dance, the acceptance of it, is mostly funded directly or indirectly by multinational and transnational media companies such as Microsoft, Time-Warner, United Artists, Walt Disney Productions, AOL, BET, Sony, Fox, Dream Works, and Viacom/MTV, who produce videos and movies with hip hop dance in the background or foreground using a push marketing strategy, which means that when people see hip hop dance they want to buy it and everything associated with it. As Halifu Osumare attests, hip hop dance "is seen as disposable art of the streets, yet simultaneously compelling, and financially lucrative" (1999, 9).

Certainly we can buy videos to teach us ballet technique, but ballet has been deemed a dance that requires correction by a live human being in order to do it "right" and I have not seen ballet being used in conjunction with the sales of products as hip hop dance is. Marketers create the "need" for hip hop dance as it is projected to and pushed on consumers culturally in and of itself and through other consumables while people are engaged in seemingly passive activities: sitting on their couches, sitting on barstools, or waiting in line in a retail store to make a purchase. The funding strategy works in such a way as to allow the sponsors of hip hop dance to increase their wealth via the media's marketing campaigns while the media increases its own. Passively received hip hop dance texts (circulating behind powerful rap music, for example) translate into demand for classes and instructional videotapes and a demand for the products hip hop dance is associated with. It has without a doubt facilitated, to some degree, a willingness to pay entrance fees to see live hip hop dance performances in theaters.

Over time, it was made clear that not everybody could do ballet, and certain movements were coded as feminine while others were coded masculine. It was and remains a dance form highly gendered in its movement vocabulary. Moreover, in order to actually execute ballet correctly, we are told it takes years of practice and instruction and then only select individuals can call themselves professionals. Even as there is developing a "hip hop body" in the studio and in professional hip hop dance, media messages are very different than that for ballet bodies. The message is that everybody can do hip hop dance if they want to; after all, it's a black thang, and it is consumed and practiced by transracially cool people. Have you ever tried to do a head-spin as done in some b-boy or b-girl moves? Have you ever tried to hold your body up on one hand, with the rest of your body parallel to the floor? Have you ever done The Runnin Man for more than three minutes or transitioned from it in into a Cabbage Patch without interruption? Many hip hop dance movements are more difficult, or at least equally as difficult, as doing *pirouettes en Pointe* or *tours en l'air* and require years of practice and training with the best hip hop "dancing masters." The virtuosity needed to perform The Sea Walk is, in my opinion, more demanding than executing *cabrioles derriere.* Just like ballet, every body cannot do hip hop dance well, no matter how much training it gets.

Ballerinas may walk around on stage with few clothes on and *danseurs* may have skin tight britches, as their gendered codification requires, but hip hop dancers don different costumes. As in videos and studios, on stage the male dancers typically wear loose fitting everyday clothing, some type of headgear, sneakers or other athletic shoes. The women wear similar clothing, although they sometimes may substitute loose fitting clothing for more snug-fitting clothing whose fabric incorporates Spandex. Women in commercial television videos and situation comedies wear very different clothing, for example biker shorts and matching tops, cut-off jeans, shorts, and so on. Of course there are the sexually explicit music videos and movies where a woman could be wearing almost nothing while standing beside a fully dressed man. The point is that the practice of hip hop dance in the studio or on the concert stage has a dress code for men and women but one that is not as gendered as in ballet. You rarely see a woman with a do-rag (she wears bandanas) and you rarely see men in Spandex. But far more of the body is covered for both sexes than in popular ballet. Hip hop dance clothes (another commodity resulting from pushing hip hop dance passively) can be purchased at hip hop clothing stores, department stores, or simply purchased from sports clothing retailers. People who perform ballet buy their clothing from specialty stores that sell mostly dancewear or purchase items online; last time I checked you could not get a pair of ballet shoes at Foot Locker.

Going into a studio to learn ballet or hip hop dance one faces a systematic appraisal of skill level before being placed into a class. The instructor gives a warmup, then a series of movement combinations and a cool down. In ballet, the names of the moves are given by the French language in which it became codified: *demi-plie, grande-plie, rond de jamb, frappe,* and so on. In hip hop, the dance moves are given by the Ebonics language, such as The Runnin Man, The Cabbage Patch, The Box Step, The Bounce, etc. Each student in each class pays a fee to learn from instructors, comes to class dressed in the appropriate attire and if good enough eventually performs choreographed dances before paying audiences.

Audiences for hip hop dance concerts are ethnically diverse. For instance, at that Illdelph Legends concert performance in Philadelphia described above, a theater holding approximately 250 people was rented and every seat was filled. Tickets were $15 and there were no seat assignments. By sight, most of the audience comprised women ranging from age 17 and up, mostly Euro American. I counted ten Euro American men, some Asian men, eight African American men and fewer African American women. Music was orchestrated on wheels of steel and the DJ was on stage with the dancers at all times; the DJ provided energy and direction for the performers. Similarly, ballet performances typically have an orchestra or music piped in; the orchestra usually sits in a pit in front of the stage where they are out of view. At the end of the performance the audience, non-ethnic generally in composition, is reminded by gestures from the ballet dancers, to acknowledge the orchestra. The audience at the hip hop dance performance did not have to be prompted to praise the DJ.

However, audiences at rap concerts where hip hop dance is incorporated into the show tend to be composed of more men. Ballet audiences in the US differ from both hip hop dance and rap music concerts featuring hip hop dance. Balletgoers are mostly composed of Euro American women of different ages. Some men do attend without having to be dragged by a woman. Research exists about audience make up for ballet performance which indicates that highly educated Euro American men and women attend. Having personally studied different aspects of ballet extensively, my experience is that few African American women and fewer African American men attend ballets.[7] To my knowledge, demographic data does not exist about the composition of hip hop dance performance audiences. At least not yet.

Far from being a dance originating with royal families, hip hop dance is undergoing the process of developing a syllabus and a canon for instruction as well as setting expectations of what to one will see in live proscenium performance. Sponsors as well as audiences are aplenty, something that cannot be so easily said for professional ballet performances nowadays. Far from being simple rump-shaking or snaking hips, hip hop dance complexity and artistry places it on par with physical attributes needed to successfully execute displays of aesthetically pleasing professional ballet. Some movements that I have already mentioned — *The Runnin Man, The Cabbage Patch, The Robot, The Pop Lock, The Snake, The Bounce, The Roger Rabbit, The Box Step, The Lean, The Knee Roll* and *The Freeze*— form the rudimentary basis of hip hop dance's movement vocabulary in codification. Staging hip hop dance in the live theater is quite different from that seen in camera-assisted media driven and televised dance. Live theater hip hop dance allows us to keep some notions of the historical documents and teachings intact, simultaneously appreciating it for its aesthetics. Surely more will be revealed.

If we saw some white children in the *cul-de-sac* doing hip hop dance we would not be surprised. As this chapter has covered, hip hop dance has moved from inner city resistance and writing to commoditized product, sought after and purchased in mass quantities. This is not to negate the fact of the dance and its importance in the broad history of life in America. More to the point it is another way to show that the new American Dream includes pieces of African America but not the whole thing.

Notes

1. In my view, the prefame and postfame classifications are ways to describe an *emic* and *etic* process, as I have already covered.

2. Positioning refers to the way in which a product or service falls within a price-quality relationship within the minds of consumers. The concept applies to both the types of performing arts instruction and places where it is consumed. All products and services, as well as places of procurement, are positioned on complex maps held in the minds of consumers. For further reading, start with Berkowitz 2003.

3. See Frith and Mueller 2003.

4. This research — development of ballet under the guise of patrons and tax deductions — has been covered extensively; see Huntington 2004.

5. See Prevots 1998; Buttitta and Witham 1982; and McDonald 1969 for discussion of the Federal Theater Project which was part of Franklin Roosevelt's 1934 Works Projects Administration.

6. See Sussman 1984; Van Dyke 1992; and Prevots 1998.

7. See DiMaggio et al. 1978; Andreason 1990; McCarthy 2001; and National Endowment for the Arts, Research Division Report #5, 2002 for a description of the historically static composition of the demographics of classical performing arts consumers.

Epilogue

Every thought we have leads to a choice. Every word we speak supports choices we make. Every action we take is a choice today which has implications on our tomorrow, next week, and next year.

> −Iyanla Vanzant,
> *Faith in the Valley: Lessons for Women on the Journey to Peace* (1996, 265)

When I was in graduate school, a visiting scholar was giving a talk about her recently published dance history and theory book during one of the seminars I had to attend. When the time for questions came up, I asked her how long it took to publish a book like hers. That question seemed to embarrass some folks, just like the times when I asked certain questions when I was a child. What I have learned is that no one can answer the question, "How long does it take to publish a book?" just like no one wants to explain, for example, why he lost that good job, or why she had that black eye, because it depends on who is asking and who is answering. The kinds of questions I have been asking throughout the course of this book in some ways are questions people can be uncomfortable with. Why does the dominant culture seek to exploit? What makes the drive for profit so great that aspects of blackness are for sale at the same time that racism remains unmitigated? How is it that hip hop dance came into being, grew to develop its own product life cycle, was marketed, whitenized, codified, and still remains a major global signifier here some 30 years later? It is not an engagement that can be ignored because this dance or some piece of it has touched the very corners of the globe.

What manner of people are these that write history with their bodies (Geertz 1993)? African Americans wrote texts about themselves to explain their world to themselves and others. Their explanations take on different disciplines spanning the unending boundaries of capitalism, using philosophy, Ebonics, feminism, and economics to theorize a space reflecting experiences of the last 600 years in America.

In this book I have danced with you from enslavement to globalization, moved you through tactics and strategies, spoke of popular women writers on the subject of femininity and masculinity, presented data from the government, and compared hip hop dance to ballet in codification and concert. I have quoted noted dance theorists and described commercials. I have discussed some recent statistics that point out reasons that African Americans have theorized their history using their bodies. Exposing some myths and pointing out ways backlashes operate, I encouraged us to continue theorizing. I have proposed that we embrace Ebonics as a tool for teaching African Americans so that the probability of commercial and material success increases for them in areas other than sports and entertainment. I have shown that our men and women suffer from misconceptions and misunderstandings and presented data that point out some of the reasons for those misunderstandings and misconceptions.

In the march and meter of capitalism, many people of difference have been marked by the dismay of consumerism and their inability to attain control over the means of production. At the same time large commercial markets exist that seek to allow the sale of representations of blackness a fleeting existence on non-black bodies. Through a variety of experiences and exploits, one can be black for a day, constructing a social identity, without having to understand the significance and consequences of racism and patriarchy that are part and parcel of the package of capitalism.

Then I argued that hip hop dance seeks, through multinational conglomerates, ways of being codified and commoditized. That there is developing a hip hop dance body that is not necessarily brown or black but that is being appropriated through practices of placing hip hop dance in studios, dance recitals, instruction videos, media representations and the World Wide Web. You can take a hip hop dance class in suburbia, or learn to dance in the privacy of your own home far removed from the ghetto streets of inner cities and the history that led to it.

Reasons for writing this book were numerous with one of them being to change the way black people are read. But my overriding motivation was that when we are long dead and gone, and hip hop dance has evolved into something unrecognizable as an African American creative text, that there is a document of this sort that survives providing information about hip hop dance as a cultural artifact, from whence it came and where it went. Yes, I have agreed that many people are oppressed and hurting from the sting of capitalism and its offspring sexism and racism. But African Americans are uniquely qualified to write about the sting given our history. That is what hip hop dance as text does.

Much more needs to be said about hip hop dance, the state of racism and sexism not just in the US but in other places around the planet, African Americans engaged in life, the numbing that occurs when we get a secure job, and whether hip hop dance projections are just new forms of Jim Crow or blackface denigrations of black people. We need to see how many hip hop dance projects received national funding from the likes of the National Endowment for the Arts and the Ford Foundation, and of those that did, how many of the recipients were African American. That information needs to be compared to historical funding patterns to see what changes have been had in opinions surrounding the funding of African American dance. It would be revealing too to discover quantitatively the extent to which hip hop dance has influenced media messages and the elaborations, felt needs, and changes in real attitudes towards blacks.

In terms of dance history and scholarship, I think working with hip hop dance goes a long way to diffusing the beliefs about dance as being an ephemeral and freedom seeking activity. But more work is needed here too. Dance by African Americans has been historically bastardized, seen and described as actions executed to please or entertain someone else. It has been said that African Americans dance to let off emotional stress resulting from all manner of constriction. Dancing also conveyed "we's happy." These interpretative points of view may have a place. I do not deny that dancing can be a very liberating activity, good for what ails you.

However, dance also serves us as a language with specific codes and meanings such that readers familiar with them can understand what is being said or what is being theorized. This type of theorizing and reading is very different from a ballet that seeks to tell a prefabricated story about a girl and a boy, or a story about gods and goddesses. Dance, and uncommercialized hip hop dance in particular, offers us ways to develop new avenues for interpreting, tactically working through, resisting, changing and writing about our condition, not to mention reflecting back to the dominant a text about himself. I use "himself" here purposefully, understanding that this is still very much a (white) man's world that we live in.

Hip hop dance will most likely go the way of jazz and tap. People know about these dances and you can still get a good workout from taking classes at the local studio or university. You can still see them sometimes on stages and in movies, but not as much as you could in their hey-day. They are outdated, not able to earn profit for capitalists. One day hip hop dance might go out of style. But I believe that African Americans will once again theorize with the next globally accepted dance text. What that will look like is hard to say. But it is sure to have elements of hip hop dance somewhere in it.

I have learned major lessons in writing this book. First of all it was not easy. Doubts and fears crept in and I often felt like I had nothing to say that was not already known. And in some ways I think that is true. However "known" and "said out loud" can often be two distinct matters. Second, I know that I do not know. We learn to pretend to know facts and figures or interpretations so that we can make arguments and come up with theories. All I really have are my experiences and what I think about them in relation to what others have thought about theirs. Third, I know that there is material that could be drawn upon in a way that would ensure I would never finish writing a manuscript. In combination then, these lessons formed a single lesson in humility for me.

One of the most important lessons, well equally important anyway, is that I am still me: black female educated other. When I begin the process of writing about marketing African American culture, or the book on consumption, or the book about the extinction of classical ballet as a consumption object, I will keep these lessons in mind, knowing that I will learn several more that will again have zero effect on the fundamental me of my body.

Bibliography

Books and Articles

Aaker, Jennifer L., Anne M. Brumbaugh, and Sonya A. Grier. "Nontarget Markets and Viewer Distinctiveness: The Impact of Target Marketing on Advertising Attitudes." *Journal of Consumer Psychology* 9, no. 3 (2000): 127–140.

Ajzen, I., and M. Fishbein. *Understanding Attitudes and Predicting Social Behavior.* Upper Saddle River, NJ: Prentice-Hall, 1980.

Allen, Patricia, and Sandra Harmond. *Getting to I Do.* New York: Morrow, William, 1995.

Anderson, Benedict. *Imagined Communities,* New York: Verso, 1991.

Andreasen, A,, and R.W. Belk. "Predictors of Attendance at the Performing Arts," *Journal of Consumer Research* 7, no. 2 (1980): 112.

Andreasen, A. *Expanding the Audience for the Performing Arts.* Washington, DC: Seven Locks Press, 1990.

_____. "Revisiting the Disadvantaged: Old Lessons and New Problems." *Journal of Public Policy & Marketing* 12, no. 2 (1993): 270–276.

Appadurai, Arjun. *Modernity at Large: Cultural Dimension of Globalization.* Minneapolis: Minnesota University Press, 1996.

Asante, Kariamu Welsh, ed. *African Dance: An Artistic, Historical, and Philosophical Inquiry.* Trenton, NJ: Africa World Press, 1998.

Austin, J. L. *How to do Things with Words.* Cambridge: Harvard University Press, 1962.

Bagozzi, R. P., and U. Dholakia. "Goal Setting and Goal Striving in Consumer Behavior." *Journal of Marketing* 63 (1999): 19–32.

Banes, Sally. *Writing Dancing in the Age of Postmodernism,* Middletown, CT: Wesleyan University Press, 1994

Barthes, Roland, and Stephen Heath, trans. *Image Music Text.* New York: Hill and Wang, 1977.

Baugh, John. *Beyond Ebonics: Linguistic Pride and Racial Prejudice.* New York: Oxford University Press, 2000.

_____. *Out of the Mouths of Slaves.* Austin, TX: University of Texas Press, 1999.

Baumol, W., and W. Bowen. *Performing Arts — the Economic Dilemma,* New York: MIT Press, 1966.

Bibliography

Berkowitz, Eric N., et al. *Marketing*. 7th ed. Irwin/McGraw Hill: Boston, 2003.

Bourdois, Philippe. *In Search of Respect; Selling Crack in El Barrio*. New York: Cambridge University Press, 1995.

Brown, Greta Griffith. *Negro Dance in America: A Revelation*. Master's Thesis, University of California, Los Angeles, 1971.

Brumbaugh, Anne M. "Source and Nonsource Cues in Advertising and Their Effects on the Activation of Cultural and Subcultural Knowledge on the Route to Persuasion." *Journal of Consumer Research* 29 (September 2002): 258–269.

Buttitta, Tony, and Barry Witham. *Uncle Sam Presents: A Memoir of the Federal Theatre 1935–1939*. Philadelphia: University of Pennsylvania Press, 1982.

Cass, Joan. *Dancing through History*. Englewood Cliffs, NJ: Prentice Hall, 1993.

Castaldi, Francesca. *Choreographies of African Identities: Negritude, Dance, and the National Ballet of Senegal*. Chicago: University of Illinois Press, 2006

Christian, Barbara. "The Race for Theory." In *The Nature and Context of Minority Discourse*, edited by Abdul R. JanMohamed and David Lloyd, 37–49. New York: Oxford University Press, 1990.

Clarkson, Thomas. *An Essay on the Impolicy of the African Slave Trade In Two Parts*. Philadelphia: Books for Libraries Press, 1971.

_____. *An Essay on the Slavery and Commerce of the Human Species, Particularly the African*, London, printed: Philadelphia: re-printed by Joseph Crukshank, in Market-Street, between Second and Third-Streets, 1786.

Clifford, James. *The Predicament of Culture*. Cambridge, MA: Harvard University Press, 1988.

Cohen-Stratyner, B. "Social Dance: Contexts and Definitions." *Dance Research Journal* 33, no. 2 (Winter 2001): 121–123.

Colbert, Francois. *Marketing Culture and the Arts*. 2nd ed. Montreal: Chair in Arts Management, Ecole des Hautes Etudes Commerciales, 2001.

Collins, Patricia Hill. *From Black Power to Hip Hop: Racism, Nationalism, and Feminism*. Philadelphia: Temple University Press, 2006.

Collins, Patricia Hill. "Social Construction of Black Feminist Thought." In *The Black Feminist Reader*, edited by Joy James and T. Denean Sharpley-Whiting. Malden, MA: Blackwell, 2000.

_____. *Black Feminist Thought: Knowledge, Consciousness, and the Politics of Empowerment*. London: HarperCollins Academic, 1991.

Costa, J. "The Social Organization of Consumer Behavior." In *Contemporary Marketing and Consumer Behavior: An Anthropological Sourcebook*, edited by J. Sherry, 213–244. Thousand Oaks, CA: Sage, 1995.

Cowley, Malcolm, ed. *Adventures of an African Slaver; Being a True Account of the Life of Captain Theodore Canot, Trader in Gold, Ivory & Slaves on the Coast of Guinea: His Own Story as told in the Year 1984 to Brantz Mayer*. New York: Albert & Charles Boni, 1928.

Crockett, D., S. Grier, and J. Williams. "Coping with Marketplace Discrimination: An Exploration of the Experiences of Black Men." *Academy of Marketing Science* 4 (2003): 1–18.

Cui, G., and P. Choudhury. "Consumer Interests and the Ethical Implications of Marketing: A Contingency Framework." *Journal of Consumer Affairs* 37, no. 2 (Winter 2003): 364–387.

D, Chuck. *Rap, Race, and Reality*. New York: Delacorte Press, 1997.

Bibliography

Davidson, Sandra. "Two Perspectives on Ice-T: 'Can't Touch Me': Musical Messages and Incitement Law." In *Bleep! Censoring Rock and Rap Music*, edited by Betty Houchin Winfield and Sandra Davidson. Westport, CT: Greenwood Press, 1999.

De Certeau, Michel. *The Practice of Everyday Life*. Berkeley, CA: University of California Press, 1984.

De Frantz, Thomas F., ed. *Dancing Many Drums: Excavations in African American Dance*. Madison: University of Wisconsin Press, 2001.

_____. "The Black Beat Made Visible: Hip Hop Dance and Body Power." In *Of the Presence of the Body: Essays on Dance and Performance Theory*, edited by Andre Lepecki, 64–81. Middletown, CT: Wesleyan University Press, 2004.

De Lauretis, Teresa. "Upping the Anti (sic) in Feminist Theory." In *Conflicts in Feminism*, edited by Marianne Hirsch and Evelyn Fox Keller, 255–270. New York and London: Routledge, 1990.

DiMaggio, P., M. Useem, and P. Brown. *Audience Studies of the Performing Arts and Museums*. Washington, DC: National Endowment for the Arts, Research Division Report #9, 1978.

De Mooij, Marieke. *Global Marketing and Advertising: Understanding Cultural Paradoxes*. Thousand Oaks, CA: Sage, 1998.

De Saussure, Ferdinand. "The Linguistic Sign." In *Semiotics: An Introductory Anthology*, edited by Robert E. Innis. Bloomington: Indiana University Press, 1985.

Desmond, Jane C. "Embodying Difference: Issues in Dance and Cultural Studies." In *Meaning in Motion: New Cultural Studies of Dance*, edited by Jane C. Desmond, 29–54. Durham, NC: Duke University Press, 1997.

Dimitriadis, Greg. "Hip hop: From Live Performance to Mediated Narrative." *Popular Music* 15, no. 2 (1996): 179–193.

Douglas, M., and B. Isherwood. *The World of Goods: Towards an Anthropology of Consumption*. New York: Routledge, 1996.

Downing, J., C. M. Judd, and M. Brauer. "Effects of Repeated Expressions on Attitude Extremity." *Journal of Personality and Social Psychology* 63, no. 1 (1992): 17–29.

Ehrlich, Gregor, and Dimitri Ehrlich. *Move the Crowd: Voices and Faces of the Hip Hop Nation*. New York: Pocket Books/MTV, 1999.

Emery, Lynne Fauley. *Black Dance in the United States from 1619 to 1970*. Washington, DC: National Press Books, 1972.

Escalas, Jennifer Edson. "African American Vernacular English in Advertising: A Sociolinguistic Study." *Advances in Consumer Research* 21 (1994): 304–309.

Ethier, K. A., and K. Deaux. "Negotiating Social Identity When Contexts Change: Maintaining Identification and Responding to Threat." *Journal of Personality and Social Psychology* 67, no. 2 (1994): 243–251.

Faludi, Susan. *Backlash: The Undeclared War Against American Women*, New York: Doubleday, 1991.

Farenga, Vincent. "Periphrasis on the Origin of Rhetoric." In *Modern Language Notes* 94 (1979): 1033–1055.

Fazio, R. H., D. M. Sanbonmatsu, M. C. Powell, and F. R. Kardes. "On the Automatic Activation of Attitudes." *Journal of Personality and Social Psychology* 50, no. 2 (1986): 229–238.

Fernando, S. H. *The New Beats: Exploring the Music, Culture and Attitudes of Hip Hop*. New York: Anchor Books, 1994.

Forehand, M. R., R. Deshpande, and A. Reed II. "Identity Salience and the Influence of Differential Activation on the Social Self-Schema on Advertising Response." *Journal of Applied Psychology* 87, no. 6 (2002): 1086–1099.

Foster, Susan Leigh. "Choreographies of Gender." *Sign* 24, no. 1 (Autumn 1998): 1–34.

_____. *Choreographing History*. Bloomington: Indiana University Press, 1995.

Foucault, Michel. "What is an author?" *Partisan Review* 4 (1975): 603–613.

_____. *Discipline and Punish: The Birth of the Prison*. New York: Vintage Books, 1977.

Franko, Mark. *The Work of Dance : Labor, Movement, and Identity in the 1930's*, Middletown, CT: Wesleyan University Press, 2002.

Friestad, M., and P. Wright. "The Persuasion Knowledge Model: How People Cope with Persuasion Attempts." *Journal of Consumer Research* 21 (1994): 1–31.

Frith, Katherine Toland, and Barbara Mueller. *Advertising and Societies: Global Issues*. New York: Peter Lang, 2003.

Gates, Henry Louis Jr. *The Signifying Monkey: A Theory of Afro-American Literary Criticism*. New York: Oxford University Press, 1988.

_____, and William L. Andrews, eds. *Pioneers of the Black Atlantic: Five Slave Narratives from the Enlightenment, 1772–1815*. New York: Counterpoint, 1998.

Geertz, Clifford. *The Interpretation of Cultures: Selected Essays*. New York: Basic Books, 1973.

George, Jennifer M., and Gareth R. Jones. *Understanding and Managing Organizational Behavior*. 4th ed. Upper Saddle River, NJ: Pearson Prentice Hall, 2005.

George, Nelson, et al. *Fresh Hip Hop Don't Stop*. New York: Random House, 1985.

George, Nelson. *hip hop America*. New York: Penguin Books, 1999.

Gilroy, Paul. *The Black Atlantic: Modernity and Double Consciousness*. Cambridge, MA: Harvard University Press, 1995.

Goldberg, M. "Correlation, Causation, and Smoking Initiation among Youths." *Journal of Advertising Research*, December 2003, 431–440.

Gottschild, Brenda Dixon. *Digging the Africanist Presence in American Performance: Dance and Other Contexts*. Westport, CT: Greenwood Press, 1996.

_____. *The Black Dancing Body: A Geography from Coon to Cool,* New York: Palgrave Macmillan, 2005.

Graff, Ellen. *Stepping Left: Dance and Politics in New York City, 1928–1942*. Durham, NC: Duke University Press, 1997.

Graham, J. *Critical Thinking in Consumer Behavior*. Upper Saddle River, NJ: Prentice Hall, 2004.

Gray, John. *Men are from Mars, Women are from Venus: A Practical Guide for Improving Communication and Getting What You Want in Your Relationships*. New York: Harper Trade, 1992.

Grayson, Kent, and Radan Martinec. "Consumer Perceptions of Iconicity and Indexicality and Their Influence on Assessments of Authentic Market Offerings." *Journal of Consumer Research* 31, September 2004, 296–312.

Greenwald, A. G., B. A. Nosek, and M. R. Banaji. "Understanding and Using the Implicit Association Test: I. An Improved Scoring Algorithm." *Journal of Personality and Social Psychology* 85, no. 2 (2003): 197–216.

Greenwald, A. G., D. E. McGhee, and J. L. K. Schwartz. "Measuring Individual Differences in Implicit Cognition: The Implicit Association Test." *Journal of Personality and Social Psychology* 74, no. 6 (1998): 1464–1480.

Grier S., and R. Deshpande. "Social Dimensions of Consumer Distinctiveness: The

Influence of Social Status on Group Identity and Advertising Persuasion." *Journal of Marketing Research* 37, 2001, 216–224.

Gripsrud, J. "High Culture Revisited." In *Cultural Theory and Popular Culture*, edited by J. Storey, 532–545. Athens: University of Georgia Press, 1998.

Hannerz, U. *Transnational Connections*. New York: Routledge, 1996.

Harris, Rennie. Personal interview, July 8, 2002.

Hartman, Saidiya V. *Scenes of Subjection: Terror, Slavery, and Self-Making in Nineteenth-Century America*. New York: Oxford University Press, 1997.

Havens, Timothy. "'It's Still a White World Out There': The Interplay of Culture and Economics in International Television Trade." *Critical Studies in Media Communication* 19, no. 4 (December 2002): 377–397.

Hazzard-Donald, Katrina. "Dance in Hip Hop Culture." In *Droppin' Science: Critical Essays on Rap Music and Hip Hop Culture*, edited by William Eric Perkins. Philadelphia: Temple University Press, 1996.

Hazzard-Gordon, Katrina. *Jookin: The Rise of Social Dance Formations in African American Culture*. Philadelphia: Temple University Press, 1990.

_____. "Dancing Under the Lash: Sociocultural Disruption, Continuity and Synthesis." In *African Dance: An Artistic, Historical, and Philosophical Inquiry*, edited by Kariamu Welsh Asante, 101–130. Trenton, NJ: Africa World Press, 1998.

Hess, Mickey. "Hip-hop Realness and the White Performer." *Critical Studies in Media Communication* 22, no. 5 (December 2005): 372–389.

Hirschman, Elizabeth C., and Ronald P. Hill. "On Human Commoditization: A Model Based Upon African-American Slavery." *Advances in Consumer Research* 26, 1999, 394–398.

Holbrook, M. B. "What is Consumer Research?" *Journal of Consumer Research* 14, 1987, 128–132.

Holbroook, Morris B., and Robert M. Schindler. "Age, Sex, and Attitude Toward the Past as Predictors of Consumers' Aesthetic Tastes for Cultural Products." *Journal of Marketing Research*, August 1994, 412–422.

Hollander, S. "Sumptuary Legislation: Demarketing by Edict." *Journal of Macromarketing*, Spring 1984.

Holt, Douglas B. "Why Do Brands Cause Trouble? A Dialectical Theory of Consumer Culture and Branding." *Journal of Consumer Research* 29 (June 2002): 70–90.

Holt, D. B. "How Consumers Consume: A Typology of Consumption Practices." *Journal of Consumer Research* 22, 1995, 1–16.

hooks, Bell. *Ain't I a Woman: Black Women and Feminism*. Boston: South End Press, 1981.

_____. *Yearning: Race, Gender and Cultural Politics*. Boston: South End Press, 1990.

_____. *Outlaw Culture, Resisting Representation.*, New York: Routledge, 1994.

_____. *Teaching to Transgress: Education as the Practice of Freedom*. New York: Routledge, 1994.

_____. "Postmodern Blackness." In *An Introduction to Cultural Theory & Popular Culture*, edited by John Storey, 417–424. Athens: University of Georgia Press, 1998.

_____. "Black Women: Shaping Feminist Theory." In *The Black Feminist Reader*, edited by Joy James and T. Denean Sharpley-Whiting. Malden, MA: Blackwell, 2000.

Horkheimer, Max, and Theodor W. Adorno. *Dialectic of Enlightenment*. New York: Continuum,1996.

Hoyer, W.D., and D.J. MacInnis. *Consumer Behavior*. 3rd ed. Boston: Houghton Mifflin, 2004.

Bibliography

Hudson, L. A., and J. Ozanne. "Alternative Ways of Seeking Knowledge in Consumer Research." *Journal of Consumer Research* 14, 1988, 508–521.

Huntington, Carla. "Ninette de Valois, Lydia Lopokova and John Maynard Keynes, III: Economics and Ballet in London 1932–1942." *Proceedings of the Society of Dance History Scholars*, Summer 2003, 55–59.

_____. "Linking Supply and Demand in the Arts." *Southern Business & Economic Review* 24, no. 2 (Summer 2004): 3–6.

_____. *Moving Beyond the Baumol and Bowen Cost Disease in Professional Ballet: A 21ˢᵗ Century Pas de Deux (Dance) of New Economic Assumptions and Dance History Perspectives.* Dissertation, University of California, Riverside, 2004.

_____. "Market Segmentation in the Performing Arts — Public Policy Questions." *Atlantic Marketing Association Proceedings* 21 (September 2005): 56–63.

_____. "Marketing Professional Ballet: A *pas de six* — Three Cases and Their Audiences, Box Office Receipts, and Patrons." *8th International Conference of Arts Management Proceedings*, edited by Francois Colbert. Montreal: International Association of Arts and Cultural Management, 2005.

_____, and Brad Kleindl. *In Transition — from Non-Profit to Entrepreneurial: Three Recent Cases of Professional Ballet Companies in the United States, Canada, and Germany.* Proceedings of the International Entrepreneurship Symposia of the University of Illinois, Chicago, July 2004.

Jackson, Jonathan David. "Improvisation in African American Vernacular Dancing." *Dance Research Journal* 33, no. 2 (Winter 2001): 40–53.

Jacoby, J., G. V. Johar, and M. Morrin. "Consumer Behavior: A Quadrennium." *Annual Review of Psychology* 49, 1998, 319–344.

James, Joy, and T. Denean Sharpley-Whiting, eds. *The Black Feminist Reader.* Malden, MA: Blackwell, 2000.

Jameson, Fredric. "Notes on Globalization." In *The Cultures of Globalization*, edited by Fredric Jameson and Masao Miyoshi, 54–77. Durham, NC: Duke University Press, 1998.

_____, and Masao Miyoshi, eds. *The Cultures of Globalization.* Durham, NC: Duke University Press, 1998.

Jordan, June. *On Call: Political Essays.* Boston: South End Press, 1985.

Kaeppler, Adrienne L. "Method and Theory in Analyzing Dance Structure with an Analysis of Tongan Dance." *Ethnomusicology* 16, no. 2 (May 1972): 173–217.

Karpinski, A., and J. L. Hilton. "Attitudes and the Implicit Association Test." *Journal of Personality and Social Psychology* 81, no. 5 (2001): 774–788.

Kassarjian, Harold H. "Consumer Behavior and Mass Communications Research: A Retrospective Commentary." *Advances in Consumer Research* 27, 2000, 100–103.

Kaufman, J. "Desperately Seeking New Audiences." *Wall Street Journal*, Eastern Edition, April 21, 2004, D10.

Kertzer, David. *Ritual, Politics and Power.* New Haven, CT: Yale University Press, 1988.

Klein, Herbert S. *The Atlantic Slave Trade: New Approaches to the Americas.* New York: Cambridge University Press, 1999.

Kleine III, R. E., and J. B. Kernan. "Contextual Influences on the Meanings Ascribed to Ordinary Consumption Objects." *Journal of Consumer Research* 18, 1991, 311–324.

Kleine, R., S. S. Kleine, and J. B. Kernan. "Mundane Consumption and the Self: A Social-Identity Perspective." *Journal of Consumer Psychology* 2, no. 3 (1993): 209–235.

Bibliography

Kotler, P. *Standing Room Only: Strategies for Marketing the Performing Arts*. Boston: Harvard Business School Press, 1997.

Krims, Adam. *Rap Music and the Poetics of Identity*. New York: Cambridge University Press, 2000.

Kristeva, Julia. *Desire in Language: A Semiotic Approach to Literature and Art*. New York: Columbia University Press, 1980.

LaBoskey, Sara. "Getting Off: Portrayals of Masculinity in Hip Hop Dance in Film." *Dance Research Journal* 33, no. 2 (Winter 2001): 112–120.

Laverie, D., R. Kleine, and S. S. Kleine. "Reexamination and Extension of Kleine, Kleine, and Kernan's Social Identity Model of Mundane Consumption: The Mediating Role of the Appraisal Process." *Journal of Consumer Research* 28, 2002, 659–669.

Lefebvre, R. C. "Theories and Models in Social Marketing." In *Handbook of Marketing and Society*, edited by P. Bloom and G. Gundlach, 506–518. Thousand Oaks, CA: Sage, 2001.

Lepecki, Andre, ed. *Of the Presence of the Body: Essays on Dance and Performance Theory*. Middletown, CT: Wesleyan University Press, 2004.

_____. "Introduction: Presence and Body in Dance and Performance Theory." In *Of the Presence of the Body: Essays on Dance and Performance Theory*, edited by Andre Lepecki, 1–12. Middletown, CT: Wesleyan University Press, 2004.

Lowe, Lisa. *Immigrant Acts*. Durham, NC: Duke University Press, 1997.

Madrigal, R. "Social Identity Effects in a Belief-Attitude-Intentions Hierarchy: Implications for Corporate Sponsorship." *Psychology & Marketing* 18, no. 2 (2001): 145–165.

Malone, Jacqui. *Steppin' on the Blues: The Visible Rhythms of African American Dance*. Champaign: University of Illinois Press, 1996.

Manning, Patrick. *Slavery and African Life: Occidental, Oriental and African Slave Trades*. New York: Cambridge University Press, 1990.

Manning, Susan. *Ecstasy and the Demon; Feminism and National Socialism in the Dances of Mary Wigman*. Berkeley, CA: University of California Press, 1993.

Marshall, Joseph Jr. *Street Soldier*. New York: Delacorte Press, 1996.

Marx, Karl. *Capital: A Critique of Political Economy*, New York: Vintage Books, 1977.

Maxwell, Richard, ed. *Culture Works: The Political Economy of Culture*, translated by Ben Fowkes. Minneapolis: University of Minnesota Press, 2001.

Mayo, Kierna. "Queen Latifah." In *Vibe Hip Hop Divas*, by the editors of *Vibe*, 51–61. New York: Three Rivers Press, 2001.

McCarthy, K. *The Performing Arts in a New Era*. Santa Monica, CA: Rand, 2001.

McDonald, Trevy, and T. Ford-Ahmed, eds. *Nature of a Sistuh — Black Women's Lived Experiences in Contemporary Culture*. Durham, NC: Carolina Academic Press, 1999.

McDonald, William F. *Federal Relief Administration and the Arts*. Columbus: Ohio State University Press, 1969.

Meyers-Levy, J., and P. Malaviya. "Consumers' Processing of Persuasive Advertisements: An Integrative Framework of Persuasion Theories." *Journal of Marketing* 63, 1999, 45–60.

Miers, Suzanne, and Martin A. Klein, eds. *Slavery and Colonial Rule in Africa*. New York: Cambridge University Press, 1999.

Miyoshi, Masao. "A Borderless World? From Colonialism to Transnationalism and the Decline of the Nation State." In *Global/Local: Cultural Production and the Transna-*

tional Imaginary, edited by Rob Wilson and Wimal Dissanyahe. Durham, NC: Duke University Press, 1996.

_____. "'Globalization,' Culture, and the University." In *The Cultures of Globalization*, edited by Fredric Jameson and Masao Miyoshi, 247–270. Durham, NC: Duke University Press, 1998.

Monaghan, Terry. "Why Study the Lindy Hop?" *Dance Research Journal* 33, no. 2 (Winter 2001): 124–127.

Moore, Sally Falk. "Social Facts and Fabrications: Customary Law on Kilimanjaro, 1880–1980." Part of the Lewis Henry Morgan Lectures, 1981, 1986.

Morgan, James C. *Slavery in the United States: Four Views*, Jefferson, NC: McFarland, 1985.

Morgan, Joan. *When Chickenheads Come Home to Roost: My Life as a Hip Hop Feminist*. New York: Simon & Schuster, 1999.

Mullings, Leith. *On Our Own Terms: Race, Class, and Gender in the Lives of African American Women*. New York: Routledge, 1997.

Mulvey, Laura. "Visual Pleasure and Narrative Cinema." In *Art After Modernism: Rethinking Representation*, edited by Brian Wallis. New York: The Museum of Contemporary Art, 1984.

Murray, J., and J. Ozanne. "The Critical Imagination: Emancipatory Interests in Consumer Research." *Journal of Consumer Research* 18, 1991, 129–144.

Mussweiler, T., S. Gabriel, and G. V. Bodenhauen. "Shifting Social Identities as a Strategy for Deflecting Threatening Social Comparisons." *Journal of Personality and Social Psychology* 97, no. 3 (2000): 398–409.

National Endowment for the Arts, Research Division Report #5, 2002.

Northrup, David, ed. *The Atlantic Slave Trade*. Boston: Heath, 1994.

Nowak, A., et al. "Society of Self: The Emergence of Collective Properties in the Self-Structure." *Psychological Review* 107, no. 1 (2000): 39–61.

Okada, Erica Mina. "Justification Effects on Consumer Choice of Hedonic and Utilitarian Goods." *Journal of Marketing Research*, February 2005, 43–53.

Orlando, Valerie. "From Rap to Rai in the Mixing Bowl: Beur Hip-Hop Culture and Banlieue Cinema in Urban France." *Journal of Popular Culture* 36, no. 3 (Winter 2003): 395–415.

Osumare, Halifu. *African Aesthetics, American Culture: Hip Hop in the Global Era*. Dissertation, University of Hawaii, 1999.

Peattie, K., S. Peattie, and P. Clarke. "Skin Cancer Prevention: Reevaluating the Public Policy Implications." *Journal of Public Policy & Marketing* 20, no. 2 (2001) 268–279.

Perry, Theresa, and Lisa Delpit, eds. *The Real Ebonics Debate: Power, Language and the Education of African American Children*. Boston: Beacon Press, 1998.

Petty, Richard E., John T. Cacioppo, and David Schumann. "Central and Peripheral Routes to Advertising Effectiveness: The Moderating Role of Involvement." *Journal of Consumer Research* 10, (September 1983): 135–146.

Pham, M. T., J. B. Cohen, J. W. Pracejus, and G. D. Hughes. "Affect monitoring and the primacy of feelings in judgment." *Journal of Consumer Research* 28, 2001, 167–189.

Potter, Russell A. *Spectacular Vernaculars: Hip Hop and the Politics of Postmodernism*. New York: SUNY Press, 1995.

Pough, Gwendolyn D. *Check It While I Wreck It: Black Womanhood, Hip Hop Culture, and the Public Sphere*. Hanover, NH: Northeastern University Press, 2004.

Bibliography

Prevots, Naima. *Dance for Export: Cultural Diplomacy and the Cold War.* Middletown, CT: Wesleyan University Press, 1998.

Radbourne, J. "Social Intervention or Market Intervention? A Problem for Governments in Promoting the Value of the Arts." *International Journal of Arts Management* 5, no. 1 (2002): 50–61.

Rentschler, R., G. Wood. "Cause related marketing: Can the arts afford not to participate?" *Services Marketing Quarterly* 22, no. 1 (2001): 57.

Richins, M. "Social Comparison and the Idealized Images of Advertising." *Journal of Consumer Research* 18, 1991, 71–83.

Ringold, D. "Social Criticisms of Target Marketing." *American Behavioral Scientist* 38, no. 4 (1995): 578–592.

Ro, Ronin. *Gangsta: Merchandising the Rhymes of Violence.* New York: St. Martin's Press, 1996.

Rose, Tricia. *Black Noise: Rap Music and Black Culture in Contemporary America.* Middletown, CT: Wesleyan University Press, 1994.

Rothschild, M. "Marketing Communications in Nonbusiness Situations or Why It's So Hard to Sell Brotherhood Like Soap." *Journal of Marketing* 43, no. 2 (1979): 11–20.

Savigliano, Marta. *Tango and the Political Economy of Passion.* Boulder, CO: Westview Press, 1995.

Schechner, Richard. *Between Theatre and Anthropology.* Philadelphia: University of Pennsylvania Press, 1985.

Scott, Anna B. "Dance." In *Culture Works: The Political Economy of Culture,* edited by Richard Maxwell, 107–130. Minneapolis: University of Minnesota Press, 2001.

Sengupta, J. G. V. Johar. "Effects of Inconsistent Attribute Information on the Predictive Value of Product Attitudes: Toward a Resolution of Opposing Perspectives." *Journal of Consumer Research* 29, 2002, 39–57.

Shaw, William. *West Side: Young Men & Hip Hop in LA.* New York: Simon & Schuster, 2000.

Sheppard, B. H., J. Hartwick, and P. R. Warshaw. "The Theory of Reasoned Action: A Meta-Analysis of Past Research with Recommendations for Modifications and Future Research." *Journal of Consumer Research* 15, 1988, 325–343.

Simonson, I., Z. Carmon, R. Dhar, A. Drolet, and S. M. Nowlis. "Consumer Research: In Search of Identity." *Annual Review of Psychology* 52, 2001, 249–275.

Sklair, Leslie. "Social Movements and Global Capitalism." In *The Cultures of Globalization,* edited by Fredric Jameson and Masao Miyoshi, 291–311. Durham, NC: Duke University Press, 1998.

Smith, Barbara, ed. *Home Girls–A Black Feminist Anthology.* New York: Kitchen Table Women of Color Press, 1983.

Smitherman, Geneva. *Black Talk: Words and Phrases from the Hood to the Amen Corner.* Boston: Houghton Mifflin, 2000.

Spears, John R. *The American Slave-Trade: An Account of its Origin, Growth and Suppression.* Detroit: Negro History Press, 1969.

Spivak, Gayatri Chakravorty. *The Post-Colonial Critic: Interviews, Strategies, Dialogues.* New York: Routledge, 1990.

Steiner, Christopher B. *African Art in Transition.* New York: Cambridge University Press, 1994.

Stole, Inger L. "Advertising." In *Culture Works; The Political Economy of Culture,* edited

Bibliography

by Richard Maxwell, Richard, 83–106. Minneapolis: University of Minnesota Press, 2001.

Storey, John. *An Introduction to Cultural Theory & Popular Culture*. Athens: University of Georgia Press, 1998.

_____, ed. *Cultural Theory & Popular Culture: A Reader*. Athens: University of Georgia Press, 1998.

Sussman, Leila. "Anatomy of the Dance Company Boom, 1958 —1980." *Dance Research Journal* 16, no. 2 (Fall 1984): 23–28.

Tambiah, Stanley J. *Magic, Science, Religion and the Scope of Rationality*. New York: Cambridge University Press, 1990.

Thompson, C. J., W. B. Locander, and H. R. Pollio. "Putting Consumer Experience Back into Consumer Research: The Philosophy and Method of Existential-Phenomenology." *Journal of Consumer Research* 16, 1989, 133–146.

Thompson, C. J. "Interpreting Consumers: A Hermeneutical Framework for Deriving Marketing Insights from the Texts of Consumers' Stories." *Journal of Marketing Research* 34, 1997, 438–455.

Thompson, Robert Farris. "Hip Hop 101." In *Droppin' Science: Critical Essays on Rap Music and Hip Hop Culture*, edited by William Eric Perkins, 211–219. Philadelphia: Temple University Press, 1996.

Thorpe, Edward. *Black Dance*. Woodstock, NY: The Overlook Press, 1989.

Trent, Barbara. "Media in a Capitalist Culture." In *The Cultures of Globalization*, edited by Fredric Jameson and Masao Miyoshi, 230–246. Durham, NC: Duke University Press, 1998.

Valdes, Mimi. "Forward." In *Vibe Hip Hop Divas*, by the editors of *Vibe*, ix–x. New York: Three Rivers Press, 2001.

Van Dyke, Jan. *Modern Dance in a Postmodern World: An Analysis of Federal Arts Funding and its Impact on the Field of Modern Dance*. Reston, VA: National Dance Association, 1992.

Vanzant, Iyanla. *Faith in the Valley: Lessons for Women on the Journey to Peace*. New York: Fireside, 1996.

_____. *Up From Here*. Taped lecture. Culver City, CA: Agape Productions, June 2001.

_____. *Up From Here: Reclaiming the Male Spirit*. New York: HarperCollins, 2002.

Veran, Cristina. "Fly Females Who Rocked the Mike in the '70s and '80s." In *Vibe Hip Hop Divas*, by the editors of *Vibe*, 5–19. New York: Three Rivers Press, 2001.

Vibe Books, *Hip Hop Divas*, New York: Three Rivers Press, 2001.

Wallerstein, Immanuel. *The Capitalist World-Economy*. Cambridge: Cambridge University Press, 1979.

_____. *Geopolitics and Geoculture: Essays on the Changing World System*. Cambridge: Cambridge University Press, 1992.

Watkins, S. Craig. *Representing Hip Hop Culture and the Production of Black Cinema*. Chicago: University of Chicago Press, 1998.

Watts, Eric King, and Mark P. Orbe. "The Spectacular Consumption of 'True' African American Culture: 'Whassup' with the Budweiser Guys?" *Critical Studies in Media Communication* 19, no. 1 (March 2002): 1–20.

Whittler, Tommy E., and Joan DiMeo. "Viewers Reactions to Racial Cues in Advertising Stimuli." *Journal of Advertising Research*, December 1991, 37–46.

Williams, Jerome D., and Kimberly Dillon Grantham. "Racial and Ethnic Identity in the Marketplace: An examination of Nonverbal and Peripheral Cues." *Advances in Consumer Research* 26, 1999, 451–454.

Willis, P. "Symbolic Creativity." In *Common Culture Symbolic Work at Play in the Everyday Cultures of the Young,* by Paul E. Willis, 1–29. Boulder, CO: Westview, 1990.

Wolff, Janet. *Resident Alien: Feminist Cultural Criticism,* New Haven, CT: Yale University Press, 1995.

Wynter, Leon E. *American Skin: Pop Culture, Big Business, and the End of White America.* New York: Crown Publishers, 2002.

Young, Charles E., and Michael Robinson. "Video Rhythms and Recall." *Journal of Advertising Research,* June–July 1989, 22–25.

Videography

American Home Entertainment. *Breaking Out—The Alcatraz Concert*, 1998.

Harkness, Jerald B., and M.J. Bowling. *Steppin.'* New York: Cinema Guild, 1992.

Hegedus, Chris, D. A. Pennebacker with David Dawkins. *Dance Black America*. Video recording. Dance Horizons Video, produced and distributed by State University of New York and Pennebaker Associates, 1990.

Julien, Isaac. *The Darker Side of Black*. Video recording. A Black Audio Film Collective production in association with Normal Films for BBC Television and the Arts Council of Great Britain; producer, Lina Gopaul; written and directed by Isaac Julien, New York, NY Filmmakers Library, 1994.

Hitch. Sony Pictures Entertainment, 2005.

Lawrence, Martin. *Nothing to Lose*. Touchstone Home Video, c 2000.

Lee, Spike. *Bamboozled*. New Line Home Video, 2000.

Mac, Bernie. *The Original Kings of Comedy* MTV Networks, 2000.

Mark, Gerald, et al. *Go Fatima*. Walt Disney Video, 1999.

Miramax Video. *Rhyme & Reason*. www.miramax.com.

O'Rourke, Dennis. *Cannibal Tours*. Video recording. Direct Cinema Unlimited, 1987.

P.S. 122 and Loisada Arts. *Alive and Kicking. Rennie Harris PureMovement: New Dance & Performance Art from P.S. 122 in New York City*. Video recording, produced and directed by Charles Dennis, New York, NY, Loisada Arts, 1998.

Robinson, Fatima, and Melissa Dishell. *Go Fatima*. Buena Vista Home Entertainment, 2000.

Rock, Chris. *Bigger and Blacker*. HBO Home Video, 1999.

Rosten, Janet. *Hip Hop Habit 3*. Video recording, produced and directed by Janet Rosten. Beverly Hills, CA: MAD Degrees Productions, 1996.

Save the Last Dance. Paramount Pictures, 2001.

Sikand, Nandini. *The Bhanga Wrap*. Video recording. Through the Looking Glass Productions; produced and directed by Nandini Sikand, San Francisco, CA: National Asian American Telecommunications Association, 1995.

Soul Food. 20th Century Fox Films, 1997.

Traffic. Universal Studios, 2000.

Discography

Brown, James. "Brand New Funky President" track on compact disc entitled *James Brown 50th Anniversary Collection*, UTV Records, September 2003.

Clinton, George. "Atomic Dog" track on compact disc entitled *Old School*, produced and distributed by Thump Records, 1993.

Cool-J, LL. "Around the Way Girl" track on compact disc entitled *Mama Said Knock You Out*, Columbia Records, 1990.

Funkadelic. "One Nation Under a Groove" track on compact disc entitled, *One Nation Under a Groove*, Priority Records, Los Angeles, 1978, 1993.

_____. "(Not Just) Knee Deep" track on compact disc entitled *Best of Old School, Phat Trax Vol. 1*, Rhino Records, 1994 (1979, Gregory Paul Productions)

Ja Rule. "Livin' it Up" track on compact disc entitled *Pain is Love*, The Island Def Jam Music Group, New York, 2001.

Mos Def. "Mathematics" track on compact disc entitled *Black on Both Sides*, Rawkus Records, 1999.

_____. "Mr. Nigga" track on compact disc entitled *Black on Both Sides*, Rawkus Records, 1999.

Notorious, B.I.G., The. "Sky's the Limit" track on compact disc entitled *Life After Death*, Bad Boy Records, New York, 1997.

Ohio Players, "Fopp" track on compact disc entitled *20th Century Masters The Best of the Ohio Players the Millennium Collection*, Mercury Records, 2000 (1974).

Parliament. "Flashlight" track on compact disc entitled *We got the Funk*, Time Life Records, 2006.

Polygram Records. *Big Phat Ones of Hip Hop, Vol. 2*, Boxtunes, islandblackmusic.com, 1996.

Smith, Will. "Just the Two of Us" track on compact disc entitled *Will Smith Rap*, Cherry Lane Music Publishing Company, Los Angeles, 1997.

Sugarhill Gang, "Rapper's Delight" track on compact disc entitled *Showdown: Sugar Hill Gang versus Grand Master Flash*, Rhino Records, 1999.

Index